# CELEBRATING DEATH

• Practice a traditional Hindu meditation technique that will build a cocoon of strength and security • Prepare for your next incarnation • Use meditation to increase the melatonin in your bloodstream and retard the aging process

And... get answers to your questions about death:

• What is the difference between clinical and biological death? • What becomes of the mind at death? • Is the human the body or the brain? (How the body or mind can operate independently of the other?) • Reincarnation—by accident or by will? • What is the ultimate secret of life and death?

# CELEBRATING DEATH

*Life after Death—Beginning or End?*

DR. JONN MUMFORD
*(Swami Anandakapila Saraswati)*
with
MEGHAN STEVENS

New Age Books

ISBN: 81-7822-155-1

First Indian Edition: Delhi, 2004

(Previously published as First Edition, Second Printing, 1999 under the title *Death: Beginning or End?—Methods of Immortality* by Llewellyn Publications, USA)



*Published by*
**NEW AGE BOOKS**
A-44 Naraina Phase-I
New Delhi-110 028 (INDIA)
Email: nab@vsnl.in
Website: www.newagebooksindia.com

*For Sale in Southeast Asia Only*

*Printed in India*
at Shri Jainendra Press
A-45 Naraina Phase-I, New Delhi-110 028

Dedicated to the memory of my friend,
John Cooper, Ph.D.,
theosophist, scholar, gentleman,
and an inspiration to all whose lives he touched.
1930–1998

*Falling asleep at last*
*I vow with all beings*
*To enjoy the dark and the silence*
*And rest in the vast unknown.*

— Robert Aitken

# Contents

# Acknowledgements

I would like to express my appreciation to The Theosophical Society in Australia for granting permission to include "Release Into Light" in my appendix. The Theosophical Society began in the nineteenth century. It is my wish, and would be the wish of my friend Dr. John Cooper, that the work of this organization continue into the twenty-first century.

Many of the quotes used in this book are courtesy of the Sun Angel quote archives URL: http://www.sun-angel.com. My grateful thanks to Stephen Bate, Webmaster, at Daily Quote provided by Technoetic (http://technoetic.com/) cosponsored by Sun Angel Innovations.

I thank Dr. Daniel Redwood for permission to quote in Chapter 3 from his interview with Dr. Elisabeth Kübler-Ross, and Robert Aitken for permission to use the poem on the dedication page from his *The Dragon Who Never Sleeps* (Berkeley, CA: Parallax Press, 1992).

My endless gratitude to Meghan Cheryl S. Stevens for her inspiration, compilation, and editing of this book, and a deep thank you to the Publishers for their marvelous design, editing, and production.

# FOREWORD

THIS BOOK IS A DISSERTATION ON DEATH and reincarnation, as expounded by a contemporary Western Master, Dr. Jonn Mumford (Swami Anandakapila Saraswati). Preparation of this book has given me a genuine understanding of reincarnation and the means to influence my future. I believe it will do the same for you.

Dr. Jonn Mumford has lived and studied in India. He was initiated by Paramahansa Satyananda Saraswati into a monastic order established in 800 A.D. He now lives and teaches in Sydney, Australia.

For more information, see Dr. Mumford's Internet Home Page at www.YogaMagik.com.

—Meghan Stevens
Mona Vale, Australia, 1997

# INTRODUCTION

THIS BOOK AROSE OUT OF A SERIES OF lectures I gave at Westgate House, Sydney, Australia, in 1986. I have attempted to maintain the momentum of the live lecture format, and my purpose is to stimulate and provoke thought, while teaching a viewpoint that is very helpful.

What I expound is based upon my own personal experience and traditional teachings transmitted to me by Dr. Swami Gitananada Giri Maharishi and others. Aside from explaining a few medical and physiological aspects, I am not at all interested in an academic viewpoint.

The evidence for survival after death has become overwhelming in the last twenty-five years and only a totally myopic scientist would fail to grasp the significance of the results.

Proof resides in data carefully accumulated over the last decade. I am particularly predisposed to the pioneering work of Elisabeth Kübler-Ross. She fearlessly and unblinkingly faced what medical doctors and scientists never examined—the psychological-psychic interface of death, and the implications for each of us!

The most valuable personal application of this book is found in the "Alchemical Laboratory" ending each chapter.

Beginning with psychological exercises, I will lead you into a traditional Hindu meditation technique that will build a cocoon of force and security. When the method is incrementally implemented by practicing the graded exercises in each chapter, you will master a life tool. Each chapter is designed to occupy a week with exercises and assimilation.

The "Gayatri" meditation will take you through the vicissitudes of life, culminating in the ultimate adventure: *transition* itself.

This is not the only way of dealing with the juxtaposition of life/death as many traditions exist; however it is a very valuable contribution that many will find suitable.

This is a book about mastering death through mastering LIFE!

—Jonn Mumford
Hong Kong, 1997

# 1

# Aspects of Death

WE ARE GOING TO DISCUSS DEATH, GENerally, and from a medical viewpoint, including its anatomical and physiological aspects. We will consider how the Eastern attitude varies from the Western attitude, and I am going to cite to you a number of very curious circumstances from my documented files.

## *Possibilities After Death*

I will suggest to you that the Eastern view of man is multi-dimensional and I will then discuss with you the possibilities of life after death. I will suggest not one possibility, but rather at least six distinct possibilities of which I can conceive.

Now, what we have done immediately is set up a dichotomy—either death is the beginning or death is the end. If death is the beginning, then I can quote from the Gita "As a man casts off worn-out garments and takes upon himself new, so the embodied soul casts off worn-out bodies and takes upon new."

On the other hand, if death is the end, then I could recite for you a Yugoslavian proverb "Life is but a flicker of flame—darkness before, darkness after."

*One life—a little gleam of Time between two Eternities.*

Carlyle
1795–1881

It is one or the other, or maybe a number of things. To understand that, you and I are going to meditate in the dark for a little while. Let us realize that you and I as human beings have pushed death out of our conscious awareness—we have sterilized it, plasticized it, and "glad"-wrapped it. In the twentieth century it is something that happens to other people—and yet the one guaranteed, inevitable event in each person's life is death.

Three hundred years ago, Daniel Defoe said: "Nothing is more certain than taxes and death." I say to you: taxes are negotiable, death is not!

## *Death Meditation*

We are going to have a meditation upon death, and you might ask what kind of meditation I have in mind? Perhaps a verse from the *Egyptian Book of the Dead*? Or you might be thinking I will suggest a passage from the greatest epic of thanatology, The *Tibetan Book of the Dead*? Not at all—we will be completely contemporary.

We are going to meditate on death for the 1970s and the 1980s with one of the great lyric geniuses of The Doors. If you have the music, I want you in a moment to close your eyes and listen to Jim Morrison's "My friend, my only friend the end"; otherwise just think about my discussion on it.

The words of this song carry the whole mystery of your existence and my existence, of birth, the inevitableness of death, of Kundalini the snake! Just let yourself drift—listening to the words. It is all in the title "My friend, my only friend the end," the opening music to Francis Ford Coppola's film *Apocalypse Now*.

Morrison's words, "my friend the end," tell us that our true source of peace is in death. "The west is best" is a reference to the setting sun, symbolizing dying as the best part of life.

He refers to the insanity of life, where we are always longing for something better, when he refers to all the children being insane and waiting for the summer rain. He sings about riding the snake to an ancient lake, which is a reference to Kundalini. Later he states that the snake is love, the snake is old, and his skin is cold.

These thoughts culminate in the words stating that the only thing that will stand is the end, leading us to the conclusion that dying and how we die are the only things that have meaning or importance in existence.

Now if you have the music, listen to it—otherwise close your eyes and consider the words "Death—My friend, my only friend the end."

To me that is a death meditation. Jim Morrison was what I would call a thantophile, a lover of death, one who is driven by Thanatos. The death force was greater for him than the life force—beyond a doubt he was also a genius.

In one of his songs he wrote "Come on, let's break on through to the Other Side." From this another group took their cue with a song titled "I'll see you on the dark side of the Moon."

In Morrison's biography, which some of you may enjoy reading, take note of the words of another song, because it is true for you, me, and everyone else reading this book. *No One Here Gets Out Alive* was written by Jerry Hopkins and Danny Sugerman (New York: Warner Books, 1995). It is brilliant!

In 1982 the Australian Broadcasting Corporation (ABC ) had a program with an equally brilliant title, "When I die, will I be dead?" We are now going to answer that very question.

I will suggest two things to you: (1) from an Eastern viewpoint, the concept of death doesn't exist; and (2) it just depends on what you mean by dead.

## Alchemy Laboratory — Phase 1

### Who Are You?

Let us begin by discovering who you are!

Self-examination is essential to form a core of personal understanding and equanimity that can survive personal tragedy and death itself. This is not a process about dying—rather this is a process about living!

We will utilize what psychologists sometimes call the 5Ls or Five Lists.

The next five Alchemical Laboratories will be the most important stock-taking exercises of your life.

We can manage to get through our whole life without ever discovering who we are, and the tragedy may be that it can suddenly be too late.

Someone wrote a poem that went something like this:

*First I was dying to get into High School,*
*Then I was dying to get into University,*
*Then I was dying to get a job,*
*And then I was dying to get married,*
*And then I was dying to have children,*
*And then I was dying to go back to work,*
*And then I was dying to retire,*
*And now I am just "dying."*

—W.G.P.

The exercises we are about to embark on are very serious and should be done at the end of each chapter before proceeding to the next chapter. I suggest you use a pencil and eraser when doing all the writing exercises.

## Create a "Likes" List

Fill the entire page with a list (in detail) of everything that you LIKE!

Don't get confused between "What you would like" (e.g., winning the lottery), and "What you like." "What you like" means achievable, tangible activities, and things that can exist, or potentially exist, in your environment NOW!

"What You Like" represents the unique preferences that make *you* in this incarnation.

I am talking about real and concrete likes—what gives you pleasure? Enjoyment? What are the things you consider rewards that you look forward to? What constitutes a treat for you? Hot curries, water skiing, painting, parties, nice clothing, reading, and so forth. Make the list very full and detailed.

## My Personal "Likes" List

## *The Inner Chat Room — 1*

Dr. Elisabeth Kübler-Ross spent several decades becoming intimately involved with her dying patients. She began to formulate some observations as a result of her experiences.

She noticed that frequently, just before death, her patients began to talk to long-dead relatives as if they were present in the room. Don't be too quick to dismiss this as hallucination!

She witnessed that as people approached death, and at death, they passed into a deep, sustained, peaceful state of meditation and acceptance. I often have observed this myself.

Immediately after death, the body assumed an "aura" and physical appearance of total relaxation. This also has been my experience.

*Science is the tool of the Western mind and with it more doors can be opened than with bare hands. It is part and parcel of our knowledge and obscures our insight only when it holds that the understanding given by it is the only kind there is.*

C. G. Jung
1875–1961

Dr. Kübler-Ross often spent months forming a deeply empathic relationship with the dying patient. She became aware that within minutes after the patient's transition, she suddenly felt absolutely nothing—as if the person was no longer present in the room and all that remained was an empty shell or in her words: "a cocoon!"

All I want you to do at this stage is to be aware of the above points and think about them. Some conclusions you come to may not represent a full or complete evaluation, as our tendency is to automatically trivialize everything by invoking rationality.

Several thousand years ago our Western culture became infected with the Aristotelian virus called *logic,* which has become both a blessing and a curse.

## *Meditation-Contemplation — 1*

We are about to begin an inner life journey that is intended to give you a skill for the rest of your life, and "life after life."

"Life begins with the first breath and ends with the last breath" is a cliché only equaled by "Life is breath—breath is Life." Breathing is, for the human, the most basic biological rhythm that consciousness can attach itself to, and this process of respiration goes on automatically, twenty-four hours a day, to the end of life.

Another word for dead is "expired." Many cultures felt the soul entered with the first breath of life and left with the last breath—hence the Romans often attempted to catch the essence of a dying kinsman by inhaling his last breath.

Western medicine teaches that normal respiration is fifteen to twenty breaths a minute, and the average rate of respiration is eighteen breaths per minute. A normal respiratory cycle consists of four phases:

- Inhalation (in Yoga this is called *Puraka*)
- Momentary pause or retention (Yoga terminology for this phase is *Kumbhaka*)
- Exhalation or expiration (*Rechaka*)
- Momentary pause or suspension (*Sunyaka*)

For at least a millennium, yoga has consisted of the practice of: (a) controlling and/or (b) becoming fully aware, of all four phases of the respiratory cycle, as a means of transcending the physical body and experiencing profound altered states of consciousness.

About A.D. 1200, a Yoga text called *Goraksha-Samhita* purportedly was written in India by legendary Yoga master Goraksha. He enumerated the ground rules for a magnificent meditation technique based on the respiratory cycle. This technique is called the *Gayatri So Hum*, and it is this method that we will master by incremental steps.

Gorakṣha made a stunning observation and calculation that correlates with modern knowledge. Translating his calculations into our time frame, he observed that an average full respiratory cycle takes place every four seconds, or in other words we breathe in and out about fifteen times a minute (4 x 15 = 60 seconds). He then calculated that within a full rotation of the earth (a day) we breath automatically 21,600 times (15 x 60 x 24 = 21,600).

The Yogi then noticed that the in-breath and the out-breath made a subtle subliminal sound that translated into a Mantra or power sound (more about this in subsequent chapters).

The first step in learning the technique is to begin to rest the mind by becoming conscious of your respiration—one aspect of Zen meditation is built on this principle. I am going to give you a series of exercises involving focusing the awareness upon your natural breathing cycle.

Each exercise should be done for about fifteen minutes. You can rotate the exercises across a week, doing one each day.

## Exercise One

1. With the little finger of your right hand smear the entrance to your nostrils very heavily with saliva—saliva has just the right viscosity to give you a lasting sensation of evaporation to focus on.

2. Close your eyes and observe, by feeling the evaporation and noticing the changes in your chest and abdomen, the natural ebb and flow of your breath cycle.

3. Make no attempt to control your breath or alter it in any way; just become aware of the sensation as the breath flows into the nostrils, a split-second pause, and then the breath flows out, followed by another split-second suspension, or pause.

4. Observe the whole cycle repeat itself, with the air flowing automatically into the nostrils again.

5. Each time the mind wanders, see if you can return it again by becoming conscious of the tide of the breath, and concentrating on the evaporating sensation educed by the saliva.

6. Allow yourself to relax in an ocean of breath tides: to and fro.

### Exercise Two

This time when you close your eyes and observe your uninhibited respiratory flow, notice that you can concentrate on different anatomical points that react to the breathing cycle.

1. Focus for a while around the navel and see if the belly tends to swell slightly on the inhalation, and deflate on the exhalation. Women may find the reverse: The belly contracts slightly on inhalation and expands a little on exhalation.
2. Don't try to modify anything—just be aware.
3. Focus for a while on the breastbone parallel to the heart, and see if any movement occurs at the end of inhalation or exhalation.
4. Focus on the lower sides of the rib cage and see if you notice a slight elevation on inspiration and lowering on expiration.
5. Focus on the wings on either side of the nostrils; see if you notice a slight movement.
6. Focus at the base of the throat, just above the jugular "notch," and see if you can almost imagine the breath going in and out through the throat as if a tracheotomy hole existed there.

# 2

# Medical Viewpoint of Death

FIRST OF ALL, WE WILL CONSIDER DEATH from a medical viewpoint, and then we will look at some anatomical facts.

## *Medical Death in the Eighteenth and Nineteenth Centuries*

From a medical viewpoint, death was, until the beginning of the twentieth century, a very straightforward, cut-and-dried event. By the 1950s, death had became an immensely complex topic.

To the eighteenth- or nineteenth-century physician, death meant cessation of heart beat, and of lung action or respiration.

If the heart stopped and the breathing stopped, the person was unresponsive to pinching (or stimuli) and the jaw had dropped slack with the eyes open, then death was almost a certain diagnosis.

At death, the eyes open and assume a "doll's eyes" look—when the head and the eyes move together in whatever direction the head is pushed, just like a doll's. The reflexes are absent. The classic eighteenth-nineteenth century test was to put a mirror before the mouth. If the mirror did not show fogging, then death was considered conclusive.

The diagnosis was very simple in those days, but gradually, as Western medicine's resuscitation techniques became more and more sophisticated, the line began to blur. Now we have to divide death into two categories, clinical or biological.

## *Clinical versus Biological Death*

### Diagnosis

The differential diagnosis between clinical and biological death becomes very important in today's world.

Clinical death basically means that the heart has ceased beating and that respiration has stopped. At this stage we have about three to five minutes to start pumping oxygen into the person to ventilate them and to get the heart going. Five minutes is a very rough "rule of thumb."

The implication is that if the heart isn't re-started within five minutes, thus supplying oxygen to the brain, then there is going to be some irreversible brain damage. An individual may still be revived, but he or she is going to be brain damaged!

In fact, that rule of thumb has been broken many times. The lower the body temperature, the longer time the person can go with the breathing stopped and the heart stopped, and still be resuscitated.

## Hypothermia

Remember a couple of years ago when some desperate person decided to hitch a ride on an intercontinental jet? He climbed into the little pit where the landing wheels retract. The aircraft then climbed to thirty thousand feet cruising altitude where the oxygen level is very low indeed and the temperature is below zero.

When the plane landed at the airport five hours later, a stiff chunk of ice fell out on the tarmac and bounced several times. It was our stowaway—thoroughly frozen and clinically dead—no respiration and no heart beat!

He was thawed out and successfully revived, without any consequent brain damage!

Three years ago in Sydney an infant fell into a swimming pool in the middle of winter, sank peacefully and quietly to the bottom, and it was an hour before they discovered the child. In the winter, submerged under ice-cold water for an hour, with no breath or heart beat—yet a medical team managed to resuscitate the child.

So the lower the temperature in the body when the heartbeat stops and the respiration ceases, the better the chances of reviving the patient without consequent brain damage. This is one way you get past the five-minute rule.

## Resuscitation

In hospitals people die clinically, are placed on life support machines, and all sorts of tests are done. An hour later they wake up and are okay. Sometimes they awaken in the hospital morgue—just before they are to be shipped to the friendly local undertaker for an intravenous infusion of embalming fluid. Trust me, no one gets back after embalming!

Clinical death is one division. With *clinical death*, resuscitation is possible. There is, however, a borderline, and beyond that is *biological death*.

At a very simplistic level, biological death is actual cellular disintegration, and you may be very certain that once the protein in muscle breaks down to produce a stiffening of the body called *rigor mortis* (hence our slang term for a dead body: "stiff"), biological death has occurred.

A corpse is much easier to lift once the muscle protein has started to break down and it has gone stiff—in a state of rigor mortis. Before that point—approximately four hours after death—it is like lifting a sack of potatoes. Again, at the point of rigor mortis, biological death occurs.

Two basic factors are present with biological death. The first is *irreversible brain damage*, particularly with a crushed brain—if your brain turns to the mush of your morning bran, that's it, you will never be there again, not in that body! The second criterion is *cellular death*.

## Anatomy of Death

Have those of you who have studied anatomy or physiology ever thought how many cells there are in the human body? A very crude estimate is sixty trillion cells. Biological death occurs when cells themselves begin to disintegrate or decay. Once rigor mortis sets in that is a very sure sign of cellular decay which, with our present understanding, is irreversible.

Everyone knows that a cell has an outer cell wall and a central nucleus; each cell has within it a whole organ system. Just as you and I have a liver, a heart, and an intestine, so cells have equivalent sub-units called *organelles*.

One of the most important organelles in the cells of the body is called a *lysosome*. Biologists call them *suicide bags*, because lysosomes contain an enzyme that will dissolve protein.

The function of lysosomes is to digest waste in the cell. As biological death starts, the suicide bags or lysosomes empty their contents into each of the sixty trillion cells in the body and gradually, over a period of twenty-four hours, the cells all die.

So at the point of biological death you literally dissolve in the acids released from your own cells—sixty trillion of them! Rather like washing yourself down the drain!

When that happens I do not believe even Brahma, Vishnu, or Shiva can bring you back to life in this body! Once biological death sets in, it is totally irreversible.

## Establishing Death

Is someone clinically dead or biologically dead? This becomes a very important question in hospitals. Currently, an EEG is ordered to determine if the brain is generating any electrical activity. "Flat line" EEGs and ECGs (heart activity) are a good indication of a shifting from clinical death into biological death.

In the United States, at one time, this determination was arrived at by inserting one needle into the carotid artery (which pumps blood into the brain), and another needle into the jugular vein (which drains blood away from the brain), then comparing the oxygen levels in the blood at each location.

If the oxygen level in the jugular vein was lower than the oxygen level in the carotid artery, even though there was a flat EEG, it indicated that some brain metabolism was going on. This crucial test helped to differentiate between clinical and biological death.

Once biological death sets in, to the best of our knowledge, it is irreversible.

## *Alchemy Laboratory — Phase 2*

Suppose your body is just a vehicle for you to *express* through and you can survive death! What is *you*? It is important to discover exactly what goes into the composition called you, if any chance of conscious control over your afterlife is to be established. Our incarnation can pass so quickly we miss it.

> *There are only three events in a man's life:*
> *Birth, Life, and Death:*
> *He is not conscious of being born,*
> *He dies in pain,*
> *And he Forgets to Live.*
>
> Jean De La Bruyere
> 1645–1696

We may argue, now at the end of the twentieth century, that people can remember their birth—several documented cases of hypnotic regression to birth exist. In industrialized countries, much of the pain can be taken out of the actual process leading to death. Despite these factors we are more in danger of forgetting to live than ever in history, in spite of increased life spans!

The sad condition of contemporary automatic living may be attributed, in part, to the trance-inducing properties of the media. In particular, cinema and television shroud us in a virtual reality of vicarious life—we engage in imaginary lives at the sacrifice of our own living!

Let us continue examining "Who are you?" by discovering "Who you are!"

### Create a "Dislikes" List

This list has to be as extensive as the "likes" list in Chapter 1, and should cover every aspect of your life. Items to be considered might include clothing, food, personality types, housing, entertainment, occupations, jobs, habits, politics—in fact everything. Think carefully about exactly those circumstances and conditions that you personally find annoying or distasteful.

## My Personal "Dislikes" List

## *The Inner Chat Room — 2*

The concepts I have explored with you in this chapter are very incomplete in terms of medical detail. We really don't need to understand much more once we establish a few facts about clinical death versus biological death and understand the point at which resuscitation is possible.

These words of Ovid can serve as a summary of this chapter. I am not asking you to believe this immediately—just contemplate it!

> *All things change,*
> *nothing perishes.*
>
> Ovid
> 43–18 B.C.

The moment of clinical death is important, because many people who have been resuscitated report NDEs (Near Death Experiences), and their reports have a continuity and similarity across all cultures that cannot be dismissed as merely "wiring of the brain" or "hallucination."

Neurophysiologist Peter Fenwick, in his book *The Truth in the Light* (London: Hodders/Headline, 1995), reporting on more than 300 NDEs, points out that "Brains which are disorganized (i.e. in a state of clinical death with subsequent severe oxygen deprivation) so that the consciousness is lost do not produce coherent hallucinations."

These reports include the subject being outside their own "dead" body and seeing details of the resuscitation that they could not possibly know, experience of a tunnel of light, meetings with significant people on "the other side," etc.

*Every birth is a condensation Every death is a dispersion ...*
Taoist Philosophy

Dr. Kübler-Ross notes that only one in ten people who have been revived from clinical death ever remember their experiences—in exactly the same way most people do not remember their dreams.

My intent is to expose you to a broad spectrum of concepts about death and survival emerging in the West as the twentieth century draws to a close.

## Meditation of Death

One of my students related the following:

> I have seen my death and the few minutes before it. It was during meditation, and I asked to see it—my death.
>
> I saw myself—old and dying. I was alone although there were people close by that I could have called if I had wanted to. However I was happy to be alone because all the people that *really* mattered to me were already dead or gone off on their own path (with my blessing).

I don't think I was in hospital and it felt as if I was home but that could be wishful thinking, as that part was not clear. However it was pleasant and comfortable, and people who cared for me were close by.

I knew I was dying, and for an instant I didn't want to be alone, but then I realized everything was as it should be and I decided not to call for anyone. I was comfortable and happy and could hear the people close by carrying on their lives as they should. I knew some would be unhappy when I died but not too much because it was expected.

My last thoughts as I left this life (and I was thinking very clearly) were "Well that's a job well done!" and I was extremely contented as I slipped into unconsciousness.

As I thought about the experience afterward—while still in a meditative state, I realized that it was just right—just the right way for me to die.

It was a lovely experience and a beautiful and peaceful way to die.

## *Meditation-Contemplation — 2*

The technique I am introducing you to has seldom been discussed in depth for Western casual readers. The roots of this method go back over two thousand years and may be found in sacred texts called the Upanishads. The meditation is termed a "Gayatri." A Gayatri is a special hymn, or mantra, that confers freedom from bondage: i.e. liberation from the endless wheel of blind incarnation after blind incarnation.

In my *Mind Magic Kit* (St. Paul: Llewellyn Publications, 1998) this is how I defined "Mantra":

> . . . a "Mind Tool," derived from the Sanskrit prefix Man meaning "mind." (Gr. *Menos*; L. *Mens*; English *Mental*) and the Sanskrit suffix "Tra" meaning a "tool"or an "instrument" (perhaps cognate with the English word "trowel").
>
> Another way of expressing this would be to say that a mantra is an audible or inaudible (silent) sound vibration that is used as a tool or device to Alter States of Consciousness (ASCs).

By the way, you may find the concept of an "inaudible sound vibration" a contradiction in terms? I would remind you of ultra-sonic devices (e.g. dog whistles and the physiotherapist's ultrasound instrument) and infrasound

> (e.g. pre-earthquake vibrations that small animals pick up long before the actual quake), as well as the phenomenon of sub-vocalization.
>
> Sub-vocalization is a concept that deserves a comment. Mantra yoga teaches that sound vibration has a least four levels of manifestation, i.e. audible, whispered, sub-vocal, and transcendental (molecular). I am expressing this simply with roughly equivalent English terms.

More correctly the practice we are learning is called the "Gayatri So Hum" mantra, or "Ajapa Gayatri," implying an inaudible and automatically recurring mantra that is triggered by the breath cycle.

When the Sanskrit is transliterated, the mantra appears as "So Ha," but I will always spell it "So Hum," as this better expresses the phonetic pronunciation. This Gayatri (there are several Gayatris in Hinduism) rhymes with Ho Hum, or the nursery rhyme "FEE FI FO FUM, I smell the blood of an Englishman."

Goraksha recognized that the exhaled breath makes the subliminal sound "haa" ("A" as in father) and the inhaled breath makes the subliminal sound "saa." This process occurs a minimum of 21,600 times within every twenty-four-hour cycle.

This continuous unconscious mantric vibration, often written as "Hamsa" or "Hansa," beginning at birth and ceasing at death, has special qualities.

When we consciously become aware of this mantra, it has the quality of piercing the veil between life and death, giving us the power to discern true *evil*, and rejuvenating us so that we can *live now*!

> *In the scriptures of* hatha-yoga, *the word "hamsa" frequently stands for the individual self (*Jiva*), especially in its aspect as life force (*prana*) and its external aspect, the* breath.
>
> Georg Feuerstein Ph.D.
> *Encyclopedic Dictionary of Yoga*

"Hamsa" is the divine goose (*Anser Indicus*) a beautiful white bird eulogized in the ancient Hindu scriptures as a symbol of the Soul and its ascent to heavenly realms. In the Indo-Aryan language group the original Sanskrit survives in modern times as the name of the German national airline, Lufthansa.

In the last session I introduced you to the idea of becoming consciously aware of your respiratory cycle. Now we are ready to implement a meditation procedure with the Gayatri So Hum (later in this work I will explain how "Hamsa" is converted to "So Hum").

The advantages of meditation are manifold and we need to understand that meditation alters our brain wave patterns and changes the biochemistry of our brains. Some of the proven research on meditation is so old it has been forgotten and I will give you one such example.

## *Meditation Facilitates Autohypnosis*

A paper by Dr. Engstrom "Hypnotic Susceptibility Increased by EEG Alpha Training" (*Nature Magazine*, 1970) discusses the benefits of practicing autohypnotic methods:

> Consistent practice of meditation facilitates ability to benefit from auto-hypnotic procedures. Indeed after several years practice of meditation even refractory subjects suddenly find they can achieve medium hypnotic trance states.

If you have ever struggled with the problem of giving yourself positive suggestions, the above is a wonderful piece of news that is little known. When I started practicing meditation as a young man, I could not relax enough to enjoy the benefits of a hypnotic trance. After three years, suddenly I discovered I could enter into hypnotic states with consequent benefits.

## *Meditation, Aging, and Melatonin*

Meditation appears to retard aging by increasing melatonin levels in the brain. The following is a discussion of recent research done by Greg Tooley, a doctoral candidate at Deakin University, School of Psychology (*Mind Magic Kit*, 1998):

> He [Tooley] has independently demonstrated increased levels of Melatonin in meditators in a study yet to be released in the U.S.A.
>
> This study demonstrated that Melatonin might be a specific physiological marker for meditation. Melatonin thus explains the subjective extra benefits reported by Meditators. Greg did a study with the well-known TM (Transcendental Meditation) group and another Yoga group of meditators who utilized a totally different technique. The results were exactly the same in both groups—that meditation increases Melatonin in the body with all the attendant advantages.

*The* Gayatri Soham *meditation is the* Hamsa, *or divine bird, carrying us beyond life and death into the center of the transcendental self!*

The "So Hum" meditation has all the attendant advantages of meditation, plus it is designed to increase the consciousness and ease of both living and dying.

## Beginning the Technique

1. With this technique, you sit up comfortably, in a chair, with your feet supported on a cushion, or cross-legged on a couch. It is all right to have your back supported, but leave your head free so that you will notice when you begin to nod off, which, contrary to what others tell you, is a good sign.

2. With the eyes closed, begin to consciously become aware of the breath spontaneously flowing in and the breath spontaneously flowing out. You can place your awareness on the breastbone or at the throat, or even the nostrils. Do not interfere with your breath cycle or try to control it—just *be aware!* After a few minutes you are ready to add the second step.

3. Now proceed to synchronize your inhalation and exhalation with a mental repetition of the Gayatri So Hum. Silently say "So" as your breath flows spontaneously in, and silently say "Hum" as your breath flows out.

4. Continue silent repetition of "So" (on the incoming breath) and "Hum" (on the outgoing breath) for a minimum of twenty minutes to half an hour. Anything less is useless.

Because you are sitting up, you may drop into a dreaming theta state and momentarily lose control of your neck muscles—this is a good sign! An even better sign is if you hear yourself snore—contrary to what anybody else will tell you.

Losing control of your neck muscles and/or hearing yourself snore are early signs that you are truly relaxing and letting go.

### Physical Signs and Symptoms of Successful Meditation

The following points are abstracted from my book *A Chakra & Kundalini Workbook* (St. Paul: Llewellyn Publications, 1994).

- **Relaxed Wakefulness:** Subjective contentment with warming of hands and feet, slowing of respiration, raising of GSR (galvanic skin response) threshold (indicates nervous system calm), and lowering of blood pressure

- **Dreaming:** REM (rapid eye movement) and sudden flaccidity of the neck muscles, producing head nodding, with subjective images, dream scenarios, and psychedelic color patterns

- **Deep Dreamless Sleep:** Often accompanied by snoring; it is possible to retain consciousness in this state—Yoga refers to it as *Turiya*

# 3

# DEATH AND CONSCIOUSNESS

CAN CONSCIOUSNESS SURVIVE? LET US TAKE this whole concept a step further. The question is: "When I die, will I be dead?" Can consciousness survive death?

I would suggest to you the evidence is now becoming overwhelming that under certain circumstances there is no doubt that consciousness can survive death. To understand why this is so, let us consider an Eastern viewpoint.

Supposing we contrasted a Western anatomical, physiological, mechanistic, materialistic attitude with the attitude in Yoga which is also representative of the viewpoints of Samkhya, Jainism, and Buddhism.

The Western attitude is this: a human is a body possessed of a brain, which secretes thoughts as the liver secretes bile. This is a very orthodox Western viewpoint.

## East versus West

The Eastern viewpoint and the Yogic-Tantric viewpoint are diametrically opposed to the Western. What they say in the East is that a human is a *mind* possessed of a *body* for expression on the physical plane.

*They say in the East that a human is a mind possessed of a body for expression on the physical plane.*

In Yoga, Jainism, and Samkhya there is no differentiation between organic and inorganic, between the living and the dead. First of all the Universe, for the Yogi, is filled with conscious light energy. The only thing that exists in the entire Universe is *consciousness*—in Western physics we call it energy.

When Einstein devised the equation "$E = MC^2$" (energy = mass x the speed of light squared), he was really getting close to a much more ancient Eastern concept. That Eastern concept said "a human swims in consciousness (life energy) as a goldfish swims in a bowl." And so-called matter (e.g. this chair, this floor) is only consciousness manifest in time and space.

If you have something manifested in *space* and *time* it has three dimensions. From the Yogic viewpoint that is all that matter is. This blackboard is consciousness, it has intelligence, and the only difference between it and the universe of pure consciousness is that the blackboard is manifested in the three dimensions of space and time.

## *Organic versus Inorganic*

Like many of you, I went to university and was taught biochemistry. I was taught physiology and anatomy—the fundamentals of medical science. I was taught that for something to be living, it must be possessed of at least four or five main chemical elements: carbon, oxygen, nitrogen, and hydrogen. These are the necessary chemical elements that must in greater or lesser part be present in any organic being.

I was also taught that, from the virus on up the evolutionary scale, one of the main keys to an organic living substance versus an inorganic dead substance is that it must have a DNA molecular arrangement as a core. And yet you know, from an Eastern viewpoint this is totally unnecessary.

From a philosophical viewpoint, the best we can say is that an organic existence, as we understand it, in this little section of the universe does require carbon, oxygen, hydrogen, and nitrogen, but we can't say any more.

Philosophers remember when the black swan argument was used in logic: it went something like the following.

*All swans are white birds*
*This bird is black;*
*Therefore this bird is not a swan.*

Although the above is a perfect example of an Aristotelian syllogism (its validity is dependent upon the first statement), nineteenth-century philosophers had to chuck this sample of logic out because after the discovery of Australia, it emerged that flocks of black swans existed.

We haven't discovered life in any other areas so far, and life as we know it requires carbon, oxygen, nitrogen, and hydrogen. This doesn't mean that life is made up only of these elements—it means that this is our understanding of life to date.

Supposing one held a viewpoint (as they have in Yoga) that the universe is nothing but consciousness — is nothing but life. You don't need RNA messenger with DNA because if the Universe is consciousness, if it is mind, then that *consciousness*, that *mind*, can *create* life instantly—the way our mind can create *ideas*.

It may be quite simple in this little fragment of the universe called planet Earth. It might be that if the universal mind created life, then all that RNA and DNA means is that it was the mechanism the universal mind created so that little bits of life here could go on replicating themselves without the Cosmos having to create a *new idea*. It might be that simple!

Now let's go back to something that you and I have been taught from high school biology right up to university.

## *Five Observable Characteristics of Life*

*Irritability* is when a living organism responds to stimuli. You poke the frog with a pin and it jumps, you step on a tack and you scream.

The more highly structured organisms are, the greater the degree of responses or the more complex the *reactivity.* If they are capable of *movement* they move, which is a logical extension of reactivity.

Organisms also *metabolize* (metabolize in this sense means to use oxygen and give off carbon dioxide), and metabolism involves a building up or anabolic phase.

So organisms metabolize, they use oxygen and give off carbon dioxide, and they *grow*—at least initially! You know the definition of an adult—

someone who stopped growing from top to bottom and started growing sideways.

Finally but not least, organisms are capable of *reproduction*.

## *The Matchbox Demonstration*

Now consider a box of matches. We extract one match and, although this match is made of organic matter, it is generally not considered as living—it is dead—*dead wood* to be precise!

Dead wood does not generally show evidence of irritability, movement, metabolism, growth, or reproduction—or does it?

Consider the match as we strike it. When we ignite this dead wood, note how the flame is small but growing. Now notice it is capable of *movement* along the match stem; as it moves along it is *metabolizing*, and it demonstrates *irritability* when I blow on it.

You may argue that although the match appears to manifest four of the criteria for life, nonetheless it cannot *reproduce*, and is therefore dead!

However, note that when I bring this unlit match into the flame of our ignited match, a spark occurs and flares into a flame on our unlit match—that is suspiciously like reproduction.

I am not arguing this seriously, but pointing out that you and I have been educated, and this very process of education often limits our perception. Even in Western biology the line between living and non-living matter becomes blurred—starting with the virus.

The Eastern viewpoint does not accept either organic or inorganic matter, nor is there life or death—there is only *change*. There is transformation. The universe is energy—living energy.

Matter is merely consciousness manifested in time and space.

## *Western Anatomy*

So let's go back to a purely Western anatomical viewpoint.

The essence of you and me is the human brain! Every time I look at a depiction of the human brain, with eighteen inches of spinal cord dangling down like a tadpole's tail, I think I am observing the essence, from an anatomical viewpoint, of a human being. In fact we are just great big, upright spermatozoa—walking sperms.

·The central nervous system consists of the brain and the spinal cord.

### Triggers of Biological Death

The brain is known in Tantra Yoga as *Sahasrara Chakra,* which is Sanskrit for "thousand petals," implying "countless." Sahasrara may be a reference to the countless cells composing the brain.

The brain is the central mechanism that triggers biological death. The Vedantists in India for thousands of years conceived that their own essence or consciousness is in the heart. Interestingly enough, the Tantrists have always conceived that the focus in the body, where consciousness enters and exercises command over the physical, is in the brain. The brain and the heart are interrelated, of course.

Many of you have been in India. I wonder if you ever saw those Shiva Yogis in North India walking around with a staff and a pot? That staff is actually a representation of the human spinal cord and it is called *Brahma Dandu*, (Sanskrit for "God's staff"). The vertebrae composing the spinal column represent God's staff in the temple of the body. That temple of the body includes a subsidiary shrine or temple, atop the mountain of the diaphragm—it is called the heart.

## Central Nervous System

The brain is often simplistically defined as: *A very complex organ in which all thought and some physical activity begins.*

That definition is the typically Western mechanistic one prevalent in the last two hundred years. All basic anatomical terms come from early Roman and

Greek architecture or from the alchemists of the fifteenth and sixteenth centuries, who were Rosicrucians and Masons. When you examine the root meanings of anatomical terms, you discover they are replete with esoteric meanings and represent a very *vitalistic* philosophy.

Some of you will recognize the cerebellum in the illustration below, the part of the brain that is the balance center of the body. A configuration, formed by slicing between the cerebellum parts, is called the *Arbor Vita* or Tree of Life (this is a good example of alchemical anatomical terminology). Life for a human being involves movement, and coordinated movement cannot exist without the cerebellum.

Look at this side view of the brain—if you half squint you can see an *embryo*. To the anatomists of the fifteenth and sixteenth centuries (particularly the Rosicrucian anatomists), the doctrine of *signatures* dictated "as above so below," and "as below so above." That which can be created in the womb is already embryonic in the cranial cavity—the brain is the embryonic potential of man's spiritual evolution.

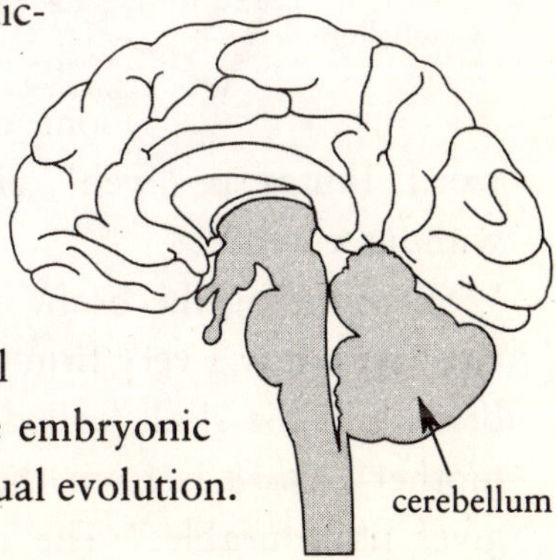

We know that we don't use a fraction of our brain! Three distinct tissues wrap the brain. The innermost layer is firmly adherent to the convolutions of the cerebral cortex, much the way a sausage is tightly wrapped in a cellophane-like material.

The first layer is called the *Pia Mater* or "Holy Mother," from the Latin *pia* (pious) and *mater* (mother). The Holy Mother envelops the spiritual embryonic potential of man enshrined within the cerebrum, or brain (see illustration here). Next to the pia mater is another lining permeated with profuse spider-like webs of blood vessels, called the *Arachnid Mater* or "spider mother."

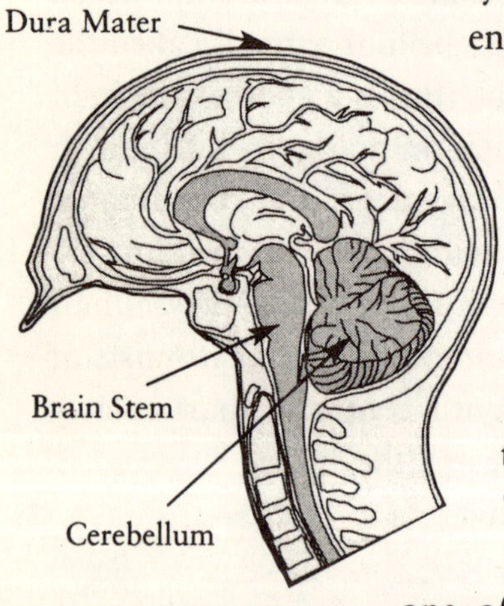


Do you know that one of the meanings of the word Tantra is "web" or "weave"—the weave without a weaver?

Surrounding the brain is an outermost protective layer. It is a very firm tissue layer between the brain and the skull, called the *Dura Mater* (hard mother). *Dura* is from the same Latin root that gives us "durable." The implication is that our psychophysical spiritual potential must be firmly protected by a hard mother if it is to be nourished and develop.

## Western Source of Consciousness

The cerebrum is the largest part of the brain and controls all conscious behavior. It is the point of origin for all motor impulses.

On the outside of the cerebrum is a quarter-inch-thick layer called the *cerebral cortex*. The cerebral cortex is the gray matter where consciousness resides.

Consciousness from our Western viewpoint is in the cerebral cortex of the cerebrum, and without this structure consciousness does not exist. The area called the brain stem includes all kinds of reflexes.

The other thing to remember is that the cerebellum is responsible for all coordinated movement. If I try to touch my fingers above my head, it is my cerebellum that allows me to do that.

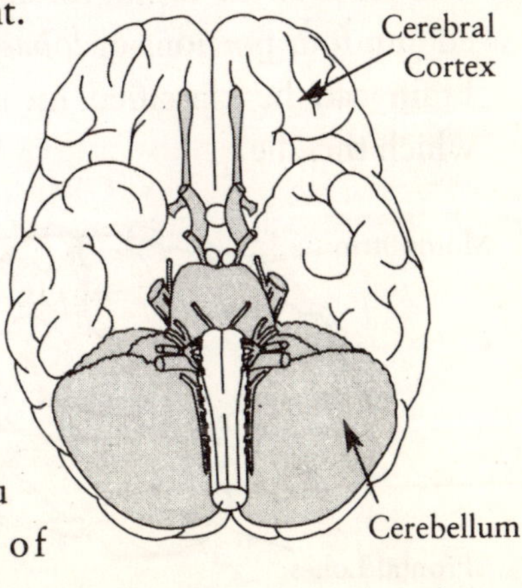


You can't walk blindfolded without your cerebellum. You can't figure skate, you can't do all kinds of coordinated activities, and you can't put one foot in front of the other in a coordinated fashion without the cerebellum.

So I ask you to remember just two things:

- That this cerebellum is essential, from a Western viewpoint, for coordinated activity. If I stand in a Yoga posture, it is my cerebellum that allows me to do so.

- Consciousness from a Western viewpoint resides in the cerebral cortex.

So let me emphasize again that, from a Western viewpoint, the outer layer of the cerebrum controls all conscious behavior.

## The Brain

The parts of the brain, for simplicity, may be divided into four portions or *lobes*. The main parts of the brain can be classified by the skull bones under which they lie.

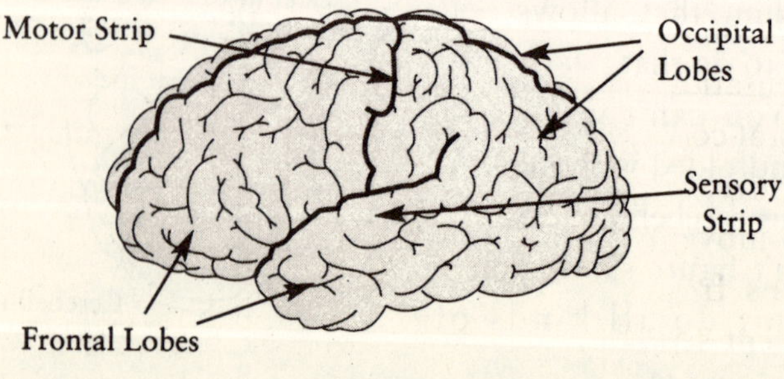

This big bone at the front is the *frontal bone*; the thick bone at the back is the *occipital bone*.

This front area shows a quarter inch of *cerebral cortex* or *gray matter* and is called the frontal lobe. In that frontal lobe, according to Western anatomy and physiology, we do our thinking, we make our judgments, we have our morals, we have our sense of right or wrong, and we have our decision-making capacity.

At the back of this frontal lobe is a *motor strip,* which allows me to move my hands. The command originates here, I make a decision to move my hands, and it travels from this area out to my hand and I move my hand—the moving finger writes! This area is also called the *motor cortex*.

The parietal bones are these shells on the side of your head. If I ask you to clasp your hands and put them on either side of your head, then squeeze, you are actually touching your parietal bones and underneath are the parietal lobes.

There are huge silent areas in the parietal lobe but the only thing I will call to your attention is that all sensation from the skin ends up finally in the cerebral cortex in this little strip here called the *sensory strip*, or *sensory cortex*.

So movement originates in the brain and sensations from the skin are also collected in the adjacent sensory strip. Thus, I stand on a tack, a little electrical signal pops in the sensory strip and I yelp. However, faster than I can yelp, a motor signal is going down that tells me to move my foot away.

Some of you who know your anatomy and physiology will realize that this kind of reflex occurs faster than conscious thought—in fact by the time I am saying "Ouch!" I have already moved.

Did you ever touch a hot iron and discover your fingers are jerked away before you feel the pain of the burn? So jerking your hand away exceeds the speed of the sensation being recognized as hot and far exceeds the intellectual process that tells you to put the finger under a cold water tap.

So we have a kind of input that is registered in the brain, but which exceeds the speed of conscious thought and awareness of sensation.

*All of the body is in the mind but not all the mind is in the body.*

Swami Rama

The occipital lobe is where you actually end up seeing, where visual input is actually interpreted into a pattern, and where you get pictures.

All you really need to remember is that the cerebral cortex is where consciousness resides as best we know, where conscious movement originates from, and awareness is registered of incoming skin sensations.

Also recall that at the back of the brain is a portion called the cerebellum, which allows all coordinated movements, particularly of the hands and the feet, including the ability to negotiate intricate movements.

Finally, keep in mind that in the area where the frontal bone (forehead bone) joins the parietal bone (bones forming the side dome of the skull), there is underneath this point a strip that allows us to make decisions about movements—not the actual movement, but to decide to move. Second, an-other strip, behind the motor strip, receives impulses conveying sensations from skin, muscle, and bone. The quarter-inch strip that overlies the cerebrum, called the *cerebral cortex* according to Western anatomy, is solely responsible for consciousness.

*Our ambition should be to rule ourselves, the true kingdom for each one of us; and true progress is to know more, and be more, and to do more.*

Lubbock
1834–1913

However, the Eastern teaching, according to Swami Rama, is that "all of the body is in the mind but not all the mind is in the body."

## *Survival of Consciousness*

When you consider this information, what was the original conclusion, or what was the original question or statement I made?

> *We are always beginning to live, but are never living.*
>
> Manilius
> fl. A.D. 100

I said that consciousness can and does survive the impact of death, and that the evidence for that has become monumental in the last ten years.

So let's look at that concept. In Chapter 4 I am going to share with you information I have gathered over the years, and discuss some experiences I have had.

## *Alchemy Laboratory — Phase 3*

It is very important that you do not reference back to what you have written in prior chapters when you are making your lists. After Chapter 5 you can make comparisons—and a great many insights will occur as a total picture emerges—the jigsaw or fabric of your being will begin to unfold.

### The "Strengths" List

A detailed assessment of your strong points is required—it may encompass physical, emotional, educational, vocational, and character aspects.

This could also include a list of things you have done that you are proud of. The list might encompass:

- Actions that have helped others, including your friends, family, and associates
- Allocation of time or materials to the community
- Contributions to your profession or your work place

"Man know thyself" was the injunction over the entrance to the Oracle of Delphi. Socrates stated that: "The unexamined life is not worth living," and I am going to suggest that the precursor to dying consciously is living consciously.

## My Personal "Strengths" List

## *The Inner Chat Room — 3*

In 1995, Dr. Daniel Redwood, D.C., interviewed Elisabeth Kübler-Ross M.D. for Health World Online. The following is an extract from that interview which I have selected because it emphasizes the importance of what I am asking you to do with the "Lists." When you complete Chapter 7, refer back to this section again.

> It only depends how you have lived. If you have lived fully, then you have no regrets, because you have done the best you can do. If you made lots of goofs—much better to have made lots of goofs than not to have lived at all. The saddest people I see die are people who had parents who said: "Oh, I would be so proud if I can say my son, the doctor." They think they can buy love by doing what mom tells them to do and what dad tells them to do. They never listen to their own dreams. And they look back and say, "I made a good living but I never lived." That, to me, is the saddest way to live.
>
> That's why I tell people, and I really mean it literally, if you're not doing something that really turns you on, do something that does turn you on, and you will be provided for to survive. Those people die with a sense of achievement, of priding themselves that they had the guts to do it.

## Meditation for Life

The following is an excellent example of how meditation can literally save your life! This was experienced by one of my students who had been meditating regularly for some years.

> I was scuba diving in winter and divers are always more accident prone in cold water I was later told.
>
> I was moving down the anchor rope with my "buddies" when I found myself unable to equalize my ears so I stopped—realizing it was too dangerous to continue. The visibility was poor and the water deep so I could not see the bottom or judge where I was and my buddies had (wrongly) gone ahead and left me.
>
> Unfortunately, at that moment a wave swept the boat away, taking the anchor rope, my only point of reference, with it.
>
> I was unable to tell whether I was moving up or down when suddenly everything started spinning, and for a moment I thought I was in a whirlpool. However, without knowing what was happening, I realized there had not been a whirlpool a moment before so it was unlikely there was one now.
>
> I could see my outstretched arms but as I tried to move my hand to the emergency inflation button on my vest, I knew that I was losing consciousness.

Realizing that I could not survive unconsciousness underwater—the regulator would fall out of my mouth—concentrated on meditating to maintain a glimmer of consciousness. My meditation mantra was:

"Hold in the regulator and breathe . . . hold in the regulator and breathe."

I lost awareness in every other part of my body but my mouth where I felt my teeth holding the regulator and my breath flowing in and out—there was literally nothing else!

I don't know how long I was in this state but eventually my buddies found me and took me to the surface.

I had serious damage to my inner ear, the balance system and the associated nerves to the brain. The specialist doctors stated that they had never seen such severe damage and initially did not believe the results of their own tests. However they stated it was not that this accident had never happened before but I was the only one to survive it.

I would not have survived without meditation.

## Meditation-Contemplation — 3

The *Hamsa* is the pure transcendent self, beyond the physical, psychic, emotional, and mental aspects of ourselves. The Gayatri So Hum facilitates us merging with our true inner being—and in so doing we merge with the Universe. When you unite with the Hamsa (also called the *Jiva, Atman,* or *Purusha*, depending upon which school of classical Indian philosophy you are referencing), a deathless and birthless reality emerges and the struggle to become converts to simply being.

*The snow goose need not bathe to make itself white. Neither need you do anything but be yourself.*

attributed to Lao-tse

We are now ready to integrate the last factor into the composite meditation I am teaching you. This involves moving the *left ring finger* toward the fleshy pad at the base of the thumb as the breath flows in, and moving it away as the breath flows out.

Why the left hand? We use the left hand because we want to ensure a slight initial dominance, or at least a direct contact, with the right hemisphere of our brain. The right hemisphere encourages holistic, nonverbal, spatial integrative experiences. Moving the ring finger of the left hand helps alert the sensory and movement strips in the right hemisphere, ideally encouraging our intuitive faculties.

Why the ring finger? When we focus upon the ring or third finger, we tap into a psychic and psychological inheritance that is both East and West.

The ancient Egyptians believed that a special cord or nerve ran from the ring finger directly to the heart, and many have attributed the custom of placing a wedding ring on the ring finger to this idea. Symbolically the ring finger represents the *Shiva Lingam* and the wedding ring is the *Yoni*.

Both Ayurvedic and Chinese acupuncture traditions identify a *nadi* or meridian running from the back of the ring finger and throughout the body, influencing circulation and metabolism.

> *He who knows Self as the enjoyer of the honey from the flowers of the senses, ever present within, ruler of time, goes beyond fear. For this Self is Supreme!*
>
> Upanishads
> circa 800 B.C.

Since Roman times the ring finger has been identified as the healing finger or *Digitus Medicus*, and in contemporary India it is still the preferred finger for anointing the forehead with *kumkum* powder.

The Vedic Yogic tradition relates the ring finger to the heart chakra, *Anahata*.

The fleshy pad forming the base of the thumb (Thenar eminence) directly corresponds to the *Mons Veneris*, or Venusberg—the mountain where the Goddess of Love dwells.

Note that some people prefer to begin the movement of the left ring finger toward the cushion at the base of the thumb by first assuming the *Gnana Mudra* ("OK" gesture of the underwater scuba diver), i.e. gently uniting the tip of the left forefinger with the tip of the thumb to form a circle. This often makes it easier to gently move the ring finger, particularly if you have arthritis in the fingers.

This gesture has a profound significance and in itself signals the mind to prepare for meditation and accept absorption within universal consciousness.

## Gayatri So Hum Meditation — Part 2

1. Sit up comfortably (there are no sitting down postures in Yoga—only sitting up postures). If you use a chair make sure your feet are firmly supported—a phone book wrapped in a towel makes a good footrest—pressure against the soles of the feet is *grounding* and *earthing*, producing a sensation of comfort.

   I always meditate on a couch in a cross-legged posture, and that is desirable if you are comfortable.

2. Gently place the tip of the left forefinger against the tip of the left thumb to form a circle. This often makes it easier to move the left ring finger gently toward the base of the thumb—it is not essential that the ring finger actually touch beneath the thumb.

3. Close your eyes and begin awareness of the spontaneous flow of the breath in as you mentally say "So": as the breath spontaneously exhales think "Hum."

4. Now integrate the synchronized movement of the ring finger toward the thumb on inhalation and away from the thumb base upon exhalation.

5. Every time the mind wanders, return to the mechanics of noticing the in breath and out breath, correlated with the mental repetition of "So" (in breath) and "Hum" (out breath), synchronized with the gentle movement of the left ring finger toward the thumb base on spontaneous inhalation, and away from the thumb base on spontaneous exhalation.

You will find that the left ring finger movement adds another dimension to the technique, taking up an amazing amount of slack and mental restlessness that people often experience.

When you relax enough, you may spontaneously find you have relinquished the finger movement and this is fine—you can reinstate the motion if you feel you are surfacing out of the meditation prematurely.

Anything less than half an hour is useless—I encourage students to use a timing device.

This exercise gives you the "rest of your life" for "the rest of your life!"

# 4

# Is the Person the Body or the Brain?

SO THE QUESTION IS THIS: IS A HUMAN A body possessed of a brain, secreting thought as a liver secretes bile? Or is a human a mind possessed of a body for expression on the physical plane?

These are the questions to contemplate as we proceed. According to the West, a human is merely a body possessed of a brain, secreting thought and consciousness.

## *World War II: Germany*

Let's start with World War II. In my files I have the following report. The German Medical Corps in 1944 documented two cases of pilots returning from a flight over the English Channel after bombing London, and landing their planes even though they were biologically dead on arrival. They had been so for the twenty minutes of the flight from across the channel.

The flight over the channel took about twenty minutes and when the Germans went over to bomb London, they had just enough fuel to stay over London about ten minutes before returning to bases in Germany.

Both of these German pilots had had their *cerebrum* with their *cerebral cortex* totally shot away—the top of their heads were sheered off from about the tops of their ears. They were absolutely *stone dead,* yet they landed their planes and those planes were not on automatic pilot.

As you know, to land a plane requires visual coordination to a very high degree. That means that something hung on, in a way we can't explain that just simply defies logic.

## World War II: China

Let's discuss the Japanese before they became fully involved in World War II. In 1936 Japan invaded the portion of China called Manchuria.

The Japanese reported a really bizarre incident concerning a captured Chinese youth. They had suspected and indeed had evidence that he belonged to some kind of Chinese underground movement.

Their principle was to execute by decapitation anyone they caught in subversive activities. With decapitation, in the traditional Japanese manner, the sword cut that is preferred is in the center of the neck, approximately between the third and fourth cervical vertebra.

So they had this youth tied up and he was struggling like mad. They pressed his head down, but just as the sword came down he jerked his head and the cut missed the third and fourth vertebra. It went in at the base of the occiput, above the atlas. The blade slid from the base of the skull, right through and out under the jaw, severing the head totally from the body.

Now, what that means is that the larynx was left intact, attached to the neck of body, but the head was severed (and therefore the brain) cleanly from the body.

The body, minus its head, then jumped up and ran screaming for fifty-three feet, spewing blood through the crowd before it finally collapsed. Blood, because if you chop off the head, the carotid arteries start draining all the blood out of the body.

The corpse traveled fifty-three feet, running and screaming, i.e., articulating.

Now, that starts to get a bit bizarre!

## *Arizona, USA: 1920*

One of the areas I grew up in was Tucson, Arizona. Tucson is very famous for a local graveyard called Boot Hill. Most of you have heard the expression "Die with your boots on." In the old West they buried the gun fighters with their boots on, hence Boot Hill.

A famous story is documented, which occurred in 1920 in Tucson, Arizona. A gambler was sitting in one of the saloons with his back to the door, playing cards.

Someone burst through the saloon doors and put a Colt .45 slug straight through the back of the gambling man's head. The bullet splayed out through the forehead, and by all accounts sprayed brain matter everywhere.

A Colt .45 revolver fires a lump of lead nearly a half-inch thick, fairly close in size to the tip of your thumb.

The time, it has been calculated, that it took the Colt .45 bullet to travel from the back of the skull and emerge through the front of the skull (thereby destroying the cerebrum) is one fifteen-hundredth of a second. That means that in one fifteen-hundredth of a second the man was *biologically dead* because of the damage to the neurological system.

What happened in the next couple of seconds is that, despite the fatal injury, this fellow jerked out of his seat, drew both guns, turned around, cocked the guns and fired, and then dropped over dead. It was not recorded whether he hit his assailant!

Allowing three seconds, this means that for two and ninety-nine-point-something seconds, the gambler was biologically dead, while continuing to perform highly coordinated movements.

According to our Western understanding this is not possible, and yet it happened. Remember the question: "Can consciousness survive the impact of death?" The evidence accumulates!

## *Queensland, Australia: 1939*

The case of Jack Brody at Mount Garnet, Queensland, in 1939, is very interesting.

Jack Brody was working a mine shaft with a mate. His working mate was fifty-five feet down the shaft and Jack Brody was at the top, working a windlass with a steel bar in it. He was lowering a very heavy bucket down to his mate.

Suddenly Brody's mate started to shout. The bucket had stopped descending, and the next thing he knew, blood was drip, drip, dripping down! When his mate climbed up to the top of the shaft, Brody was totally comatose—at first they thought he was dead.

Brody had been turning the windlass when it slipped and the steel bar handle flew back, crashing onto the coronal suture of his skull—the exact place where the frontal bone joins the two parietal bones.

The *sensory* and *motor cortex* is right underneath this point. The injury to Brody's crushed skull was three quarters of an inch deep, three quarters of an inch wide, and three inches across. A massive head injury!

Now so far as we know, nobody can sustain a depressed skull fracture like that and retain consciousness—or even survive! That type of damage would render the victim instantly unconscious. The injury left Brody comatose for two months and it was two years before he was released from hospital.

You can see the depressed fracture on his head in photographs. Despite his injury, he managed, without being conscious (as we would understand it), to catch the windlass in his elbow and perform a complicated maneuver in which he picked up a lock-pin and inserted it in the windlass to jam it so his mate wouldn't be killed.

From my Western understanding, that is just totally, absolutely impossible!

I do not intend to be gruesome with the following two incidents, and in fact if you are very sensitive perhaps you can skip the remainder of the chapter.

These events span geographical distances as diverse as from Nepal to Cambridge.

## *Nepal: 1984*

Dakshina Kali is one of two places left in Asia that I know of where animal sacrifice is still practiced. The other place is a temple in Calcutta. Calcutta was originally called "Kali cut," that is "place of sacrifice to Kali." At a certain shrine in Calcutta, once a year a bull is sacrificed.

In Dakshina Kali, outside Katmandu, twice a week, on Tuesday and Saturday, a sacrifice is made to the Goddess Kali.

Here you may bring an egg, hen, dog, goat, or bull (for the wealthy); these arc the preferred sacrifices. That place has about it one of the most, for me personally, evil atmospheres that I have ever experienced.

I observed and photographed a goat being sacrificed by the priests. They twisted its head back and slit the animal's throat, letting the carotid arteries spurt blood onto a statue of Kali. When the blood was completely drained from the goat's body they finished severing the head from the body.

The goat's body was laid down, with the priest standing on its fore legs and hind legs because the creature was still capable of getting up and running.

The tail was cut off and stuffed in the goat's mouth, because they believe that if the goat continues to squeal it is a bad omen, and they then proceeded to put the goat's head at the rear of the animal's body—near where the tail was severed from it.

The object of that sacrifice, by the way, is that one makes a wish, offers an egg, a hen, a dog, or a goat as a sacrifice, and Kali will make that wish true. The Nepalese queue up by the hundreds at the Kali temples with their sacrificial offerings, twice a week.

Now why did I tell you this story? Remember, I said that two things are required. For coordinated movement you need the cerebellum, and you need consciousness in the cerebral cortex.

## *Cambridge, Britain: 1961*

I was not there to personally verify the following anecdote. In 1961 my book *Psychosomatic Yoga* was published in London. I came over to Australia on a ship with a young Cambridge veterinarian who was a good friend of mine for a few years, although I must say he was one of the most obnoxious people that I have ever met. We will call him Sebastian.

About eight years ago, when I gave this lecture in Cairns, somebody attending the lecture had actually been up in New Guinea with me and verified knowing Sebastian. Sebastian was an extremely skeptical and hardheaded fellow, and he and I sat up many a night drinking and having arguments. I showed him a number of things to do with Yoga and he shared a lot with me. He told me about a personal experience he had at Cambridge. If you had known Sebastian then you could not have met anyone more skeptical, cynical, and hardheaded.

At Cambridge University, a group of students were interested in what some of you may know as telekinesis. Telekinesis is the ability of the mind to influence an animate or inanimate object without any physical contact.

What these students did while Sebastian was there was to decapitate a bulldog. They cut its head off. They put the dog's head on a table, four feet away from the body, and allowed the carotid arteries to drain all the blood out of the body.

Within a minute all the blood was totally drained from the body. Remember that the dog's head is *four feet* away, and that along with that dog's head goes its cerebellum!

The students sat around in a circle using a special concentration method. After half an hour the dog stood up, walked in a series of coordinated steps over to its head, and collapsed.

Now that is not possible! According to Western science that is totally impossible. Not only is the cerebellum required for the coordinated movement of walking (I am not talking about reflexes such as knee jerks), but in order to operate, muscle requires blood. Blood transports glucose (sugar) and oxygen to the muscles. The incident is, from the viewpoint of Western science, an absolute medical impossibility.

*Millions long for immortality who do not know what to do with themselves on a rainy Sunday afternoon.*

Susan Ertz

How could such things be possible?

## *Alchemy Laboratory — Phase 4*

So far you have examined your likes, dislikes and strengths or strong points. It is very important that at this stage you do not refer back and cross-reference the lists—this you can do in Alchemy Laboratory — Phase 6.

We now want to construct a list of your weaknesses, which should include everything you consider a hindrance about yourself—such things as personality traits, physical problems, inherited tendencies, temperament, habituations, addictions and relationships. These weaknesses may be perceived or actual, real or imagined—it is not important. What is important is how you see yourself or feel about yourself.

This is all part of your self-evaluation and is not intended to arouse insecurity or negativity. Years ago we used to have a little saying: "The biggest room for improvement is the room for self-improvement." The most fertile field for exploration and development sits right on top of our shoulders! When I was young, we also used to say that the winning distance was six inches—from ear to ear!

This potential for self-monitoring and self-correction can make living a dynamic experience!

## My Personal List of "Weak Points"

## *The Inner Chat Room — 4*

The nonphysical part of a human is always perfect and whole—this aspect is often called the spiritual body, astral body, etheric body, mental body, and many other names.

People documenting near-death experiences have reported that no matter the state of the body at the moment of death (e.g. limbs amputated in an accident, or a body distorted with cerebral palsy), they sensed themselves free of the physical body—in a subtle body perfectly formed, with all limbs and functions intact.

> *The mind is no more in the body than music is in the instrument.*
>
> Robert Anton Wilson

The nonphysical categories of a human being are often collectively lumped under the term "mind" and you may begin now to realize that the evidence is substantial for the mind being separate and surviving the death of the physical body.

At this stage I only want to suggest to you that the real part of you is not only more than your physical body, but also more than your mind, or your feelings, or your memories. The real essence of being is beyond all of this.

In the next chapter we will delineate the five bodies of humans as taught in Yoga.

# *Meditation-Contemplation — 4*

## Gayatri So Hum Meditation — Part 3

Every part of this meditation that I am initiating you into speaks to the deepest and most universal realms of our collective unconscious.

The Sanskrit word Hamsa (also Hansa) is often translated as "swan," largely because the English ridiculed geese in nursery rhymes. The very beautiful Hamsa is, in fact, a most elegant goose, whose yearly migrations in India have always symbolized the spirit or soul ceaselessly moving from body to body in rounds of incarnations.

*The trouble with Western man is he does not know how to be content in an empty room!*

Pascal
Eighteenth-century French philosopher

The Hamsa is said to possess such fine powers of discernment that when drinking it can separate milk from water if the two liquids are mixed. Thus the Hamsa sips up only the snow-white milk that matches the luster of its skin, leaving behind the gross water.

Our Yoga masters, when they have reached a certain point of evolution, have this discernment so finely developed that they are given the title *Paramahamsa*— those whose souls feed only upon the purest of philosophical truths.

The mystery of how Hamsa converts to So Hum will be revealed in another chapter, but now we need to realize more about the magical ring finger or *digitus medicus*.

## The Magic Ring Finger

For several thousand years, the ring finger has been recognized as a special channel for healing and psychic energy. The best summary I could give you would be to quote Benjamin Walker, writing in his *Encyclopedia of Esoteric Man* (London: Routledge & Kegan Paul LTD, 1977):

> The ring finger, also called the leech (doctor's) finger, the digitus medicus, or physician's finger. It is the healing finger, and when stroked over a wound is believed to heal it. Medieval apothecaries used to mix their medicaments and potions with this finger. All ointments should be rubbed on with the ring finger, never the forefinger. In the Samothracian mysteries, which were celebrated in ancient times in scattered centres in the Aegean Sea, the ring finger was enclosed in a finger-stall of magnetic iron, and this "idaeic" finger (named after Mount Ida in Crete) was used in healing ceremonies. Even today rings are mostly worn on this finger, especially of the left hand, and it is called the annular, or ring-bearing finger. In palmistry it is the finger of Apollo and is related to the emotions and the arts.

## The Gnana Mudra

It is recommended that you gently join the forefinger and thumb of the left hand before commencing the ring finger movement. You are also welcome to do this with the right hand so that both hands are resting palm up, on your thighs, in the Gnana Mudra gesture. The technique is described in my book *A Chakra & Kundalini Workbook* (St. Paul: Llewellyn, 1994):

> Uniting the thumb with the index finger forms a circle in which finite, limited humanity is linked with the infinite, unlimited absolute. The circle is a (w)hole, being both absolute zero and utter completeness. Pascal, the seventeenth-century French theologian, defined God as a circle whose circumference is nowhere and center everywhere.
>
> It is incorrect to say that God exists: only humanity exists and the moment something exists it is already limited by form and name (Namarupa). God subsists and persists but never exists.

The Gayatri So Hum meditation is intended to develop a habit so strong that you can even consciously die while learning to relax anywhere and anytime. The Gayatri So Hum meditation is also flexible in that although we master it sitting up, the technique can be done lying down, provided the torso is propped up to facilitate ease of breathing.

## Meditation Tip

*The So Hum meditation is a raft upon which we may cross the ocean of life . . . the ocean of life flows into the universal ocean.*

Place a tape recorder or a note pad and pen beside you before you begin to meditate. Make a notation of the time and date.

When you are finished with the meditation make a record of any experiences, visions, ideas, sensations, feelings or insights that you may have encountered.

## Technique Summary: ARRTM

- Awareness of spontaneous
- Respiratory inspiration and expiration
- Recitation mentally of "So" on inspiration and "Hum" on expiration
- Touch together thumb and forefinger of left hand (both hands if you wish) to form Gnana Mudra
- Move gently the ring finger of the left hand toward the base of the thumb on inhalation and away on exhalation

I WOULD LI

Western

suggest

structure

I don't

cerned with

infringing any

may have.

possibilities

The idea

al beings

one body.

are a five

times known

symbols

pointed st

# 5

# THE FIVE BODIES

I WOULD LIKE TO TRANSPORT YOU FROM A Western viewpoint to an Eastern viewpoint. I will suggest to you a method of conceptualizing the structure of humans in a unique way.

I don't suggest that you have to believe or be concerned with anything I say, nor am I interested in infringing any belief, philosophy, or knowledge you may have. The scheme I will outline opens up new possibilities.

The idea is that individuals are multi-dimensional beings and, in a sense, we are not possessed of one body. As Yoga, Vedanta, and Tantra teach, we are a five-bodied being. These bodies are sometimes known as *Kosha,* or sheaths, and one of the symbols representing this is the Panchkona or five pointed star, i.e. the Pentagram.

## *Five Bodies of Eastern Philosophy*

These five bodies are:

| | |
|---|---|
| Physical Body | *Annamaya Kosha* |
| Etheric Body | *Pranamaya Kosha* |
| Astral Body | *Manamaya Kosha* |
| Mental Body | *Vijnamaya Kosha* |
| Spiritual Body | *Anandamaya Kosha* |

### Physical Body: Annamaya Kosha

The first body is called *Annamaya Kosha*. *Anna* means "food," *maya* means "form"—another spelling of maya is better known as" illusion," a different word. So Annamaya Kosha is *the food-formed sheath*. We may simply call it the physical body because the physical body is indeed built on sustenance—the nourishment we take in, be it water, food, or air. The Annamaya Kosha is the physical body that we understand so well in our Western physiology and anatomy.

### Etheric Body: Pranamaya Kosha

Behind the physical body is the *Pranamaya Kosha* or the etheric body. This etheric body is a corpus that has subtle *layers* of energy, much as a room is permeated with wiring that allows the central lights to go on. If there is any interference with that wiring, the lights go out.

The relationship between the etheric body and the physical body is rather like the relationship between the nervous system and the physical body. The etheric body is a matrix of pure energy, supporting and feeding the physical.

The etheric body provides a kind of power, a kind of spiritual energy or prana, to move the physical body, including allowing the electrical-chemical operations of the nervous system. It provides the pranic irrigation channels (*nadis*) or acupuncture meridians that nourish the physical body. It is both the substrata and the matrix supporting the physical body.

The etheric body is the subtle energy body of the *phantom limb* that amputees report. Indeed the etheric body is the *phantom body*!

## Astral or Emotional Body: Maṇamaya Kosha

Beyond that etheric body is another body. This body is known as *Manamaya Kosha*. In Western terms we would call it the *astral* or *emotional body*. This astral-emotional body is like that part of our nervous system (the limbic system and the thalamus in the brain) that is responsible for emotional reaction. It is a body that is glued together or held by emotion or feeling, both positive and negative. It has to do also with the dream world.

### Mental Body: Vijnamaya Kosha

After the astral body is the *Vijnamaya Kosha,* or the body of *discrimination.* We will call it the *mental body.* This mental body is capable of logic—it holds the *budhi* or the reasoning faculty, and is capable of pure mental computation and coming to decisions.

### Spiritual Body: Anandamaya Kosha

Finally there is the *Anandamaya Kosha*, the *spiritual body.* This is the deepest core of being—our essence, which is beyond words. More about this later.

## *Integration of the Five Bodies*

Like the five digits of the hand, this Yogic approach suggests that we have not one—but five bodies and these five bodies integrate. If we look at this idea, whether we agree with it or not, we can start to explain all kinds of things.

Let me start out with a physical analogy. What sounds like something esoteric from a Western viewpoint can immediately be translated into understandable terms.

This physical body is a conglomeration of actual tissues composed of some sixty trillion cells, stratified into organs and systems.

If you walk over to me and kick me in the shins, some nerve endings in the shinbone will fire, this is like the etheric body being brought into action.

As the pain impulses register in the limbic system of my brain (deep inside the cerebrum), I get emotional, I get shocked, I get dazed, I get confused and this activation is the astral or emotional body.

Then the impulses go up to my cerebral cortex and the frontal lobes take over. "That's got to be an accident because I haven't annoyed you," is the conclusion reached, and this is a function typical of the mental body.

The spiritual body, throughout this experience, remains totally uninvolved, functioning as merely the silent witness of my life and events.

## *Hindu View of Death*

We can actually translate the concept of psychic bodies into physical terms. However, what I am talking about is beyond the mere physical.

*Clinical death*, with cessation of heartbeat and respiration, belongs to the domain of the physical (Annamaya Kosha) body.

The Hindu conceives that clinical death, which slowly transforms into *biological death*, is the result of the etheric (Pranamaya Kosha) body separating or coming away from the physical body, and it is this that allows the biological decay of the individual cells to begin.

In India it is customary to strew the newly dead body with fresh flowers. The belief is that flowers have inherent pranic energy, and if you bury the corpse in fresh flowers you will keep the etheric body adhering to the physical body a little longer. The result is that the rate of decay is slowed so that a clean separation of the subtler bodies from the physical gross vehicle will occur at cremation.

Cremation is the second most popular method of disposing of the dead, burial being the first. Hindu cremation is based on a belief prevalent in Western alchemy—that the soul or essence of a substance is released by burning.

Western cremations, with the attendant institution of crematoriums, are a poor parody of Hindu cremations. We pollute the atmosphere with the process as the embalming fluid releases toxic mercury gas.

The etheric body, as it begins to move away from the physical body, initiates biological death. As the etheric or pranic vehicle withdraws, you start to see the phenomenon of *fairy lights*—elfin lights, the aura around the dead, floating balls of light in a graveyard, apparitions, ghosts, etc.

That astral emotional body carries our emotional reactions throughout life, and the astral body functions every night when you and I fall asleep.

When we talk about "going to the astral world," we are talking about dreaming. In the Hindu-Tibetan doctrine you dream using the astral Manamaya Kosha to move about in a world of magic and illusion—a subject we will discuss shortly.

Finally, that mental body (Vijnamaya Kosha) includes a memory storehouse which it can draw on from the astral body. This memory bank is the personal *Akashic* record of every event that ever occurred in our life.

## *Sequential Separation of the Psychic Sheaths at Death*

Once the etheric body separates from the physical there is a natural process whereby the etheric body disintegrates and the astral emotional body, the mental, and the spiritual bodies group together as a conglomerate unit.

That astral emotional body will lock you in a dream world. When the astral emotional body separates from the mental body, it gives all its emotional memories to the intellectual cognitive memories of the mental body. Under certain circumstances, at death, it would appear that many of the ten billion cells of the cerebral cortex discharge and that your whole life is reviewed.

When you read my forthcoming book *The Karma Manual: 9 Days to Clear Your Karma* (St. Paul: Llewellyn Publications, 1999), you will learn the Karma Shakti Kriya technique: to review your life every night as you fall asleep. In certain types of death—drowning particularly—and sometimes in a car accident, where there are a few seconds of foreknowledge of death, an individual's whole life will pass before him or her. The cells of the cerebral cortex empty out the contents of the mental body—reviewing the individual's entire life.

Now we are left with that spiritual body. And that spiritual body, in Hindu tradition, particularly in Samkhya and Vedanta, carries within it an essence called Purusha. "Pur" means city in Sanskrit, and "sha" means to sleep.

*So it is the city within which the essence sleeps, or what we in the West would call soul*, but there is one difference. In Samkhya, Vedanta, and to the Buddhists, the pure soul, the Purusha, has no attributes, no memories of personal life. It is that Purusha that provides a motive force for life after life after life, or rebirth after rebirth. I would suggest to you that we have a misunderstanding about reincarnation.

What I have said about these bodies is just a brief introduction. Now let me put it exactly and precisely together for you. The next thing we will discuss will be the possibilities of what actually does happen at death or after death.

## *What is the Secret of Life and Death?*

It is not a question of "When I die, will I be dead?" Rather it is a question that not one thing happens but a number of things! You see, the evidence that the consciousness can survive the impact of death is accumulating all the time.

I will give you the ultimate secret of life and death! This is the ultimate and penultimate secret to take away and think about, and I would just say at this point that *as in life so in death*. If you are stupid in life, you are going to be just as stupid when you are dead! I have talked to lots of stupid dead people, and I can assure you of that.

On Sunday nights there are many spiritualist churches holding services. If you want to entertain and educate yourself without offending anyone, you can go around to every spiritualist church.

At every meeting you go to, from every voice that comes through, you will hear a different story. Some people will tell you that Jesus Christ was there when they died, and other people will inform you that we will reincarnate life after life. Others will tell you that there is a great master waiting for you, and so forth.

In other words, what these mediums are getting is a different story from each person. Since mediums have different beliefs and certain attitudes, naturally they are going to attract people who concur with their attitudes. This will become understandable as we move along in our study.

Yes, the dead can be contacted, but it is not always possible and it is not straightforward!

Did it ever occur to you that if contacting the dead were a simple procedure and you could go call up anyone you wanted the way you use a telephone, the Sharon Tate murder that occurred during the 1970s could have been solved in one hour. I just give that to you as an example!

All you would have to do if it were as simple as "hooking in" is go get a medium, contact the victim, and ask for a description of the murderer. Isn't that true? It is not very often that you hear of crimes being solved that way, so this isn't a simple matter. I am not claiming it is simple and straightforward, nor does it always happen.

## *Alchemy Laboratory — Phase 5*

If we grasp Kafka's statement and truly feel it as a truth about opportunity from womb to tomb that will cease, then we may become possessed with a divine urgency that can bring the best out in us.

> *The meaning of life is that it stops.*
>
> Franz Kafka

You have systematically defined and enumerated your Likes, Dislikes, Strengths, and Weaknesses.

Without referring back to any previous lists, I now want you to make a careful and detailed list of everything in your life that you currently perceive as a problem area. These can range from personal to financial, from work to relationships—anything whatsoever.

*After you have finished the next list* go back to your prior lists in Alchemy Laboratories 1 to 4, and see if you can identify any recurring themes or obvious similarities.

Create a "Problem" List, and then create your "Recurring Themes" List.

## My Personal "Problem" List

## My Personal "Recurring Themes" List

## The Inner Chat Room — 5

An astounding data bank of reports concerning revival from clinical death has accumulated in the last ten years. What makes these reports astounding is the coherency and consensus that appear in diverse cultures, from Eskimo to Australian Aborigine.

Consider this statement from a Norwegian engineer describing an NDE he experienced at the age of fourteen, reported by Dr. Melvin Morse, M.D. in his book *Transformed by the Light* (New York: Ivy Books, 1992, p. 11).

> Suddenly I was on the other side, and all pains were gone. I had lost all my interest and attachment to my biological life. I realized that the boundary between life and death is a strange creation of our mind. It is horrifying and real when perceived from this side (the side of the living) and yet is insignificant when perceived from the other side.
>
> My first impression was a total surprise. How could I exist in such a comfortable way and how could I perceive and think while being dead and yet have no body?

Contrast this with a report as early as 1975 by Dr. Raymond A. Moody. Jr., M.D. in *Life After Life* (New York: Bantam Books, 1977, p. 49):

When I came out of the physical body it was like I did come out of my body and go into something else. I didn't think I was just nothing. It was another body . . . but not another regular human body. It's a little bit different. It was not exactly like a human body, but it wasn't any big glob of matter, either. It had form to it, but no colors. And I know I still had something I could call hands.

# Meditation-Contemplation — 5

## Gayatri So Hum Meditation — Part 4

Let us recapitulate what we have learned about Hamsa. In *A Dictionary of Hinduism* (London: Routledge & Kegan Paul: 1977), Margaret and James Stutley observe:

> The hamsa symbolizes knowledge and the life-force or cosmic breath (prana), "ham" being its exhalation, and "sa," its inhalation which is regarded as the return of the individual life-force to brahman, its cosmic source. The lofty flight of the hamsa is therefore likened to the spiritual efforts of the devout Hindu to attain brahman.

The sound "Ham Sa" or "So Hum" is really an onomatopoetic mantric sound of the exaggerated breath in the same way that the word "gargle" is an onomatopoetic sound of the throat cleansing action.

You can get a feel for this yourself by opening your mouth and forcefully breathing out and noting at the end of the breath the spontaneous manifestation of "Haaaa." Conversely if you leave the lips slightly parted, with the tongue resting on the floor of the mouth, then sharply inhale, you will experience the audible sibilant sound "Saaaa."

Thus this mantra goes on unconsciously 21,600 times a day, from birth to death. However, Master

Goraksha discovered that it is only efficacious when we are consciously aware of manufacturing it.

His greatest discovery was electing to start the meditation with focusing on the in breath first so that the mantric pattern is "So Hum." This was quite a deliberate choice.

## The Ultimate Secret of the Gayatri So Hum

In Sanskrit the phrase for merging with the absolute is "So Ham," which literally means "He (So) I am" (Ham): *He I am* is the ultimate affirmation of wholeness and integration with the cosmic consciousness and he who practices the Gayatri So Hum is consciously affirming union and oneness—each inhalation and exhalation deepens our tendency toward melting into one single harmonic often called the Uni-Verse.

> *The Spirit is beyond sound and form, without touch and taste and perfume. It is eternal, unchangeable, and without beginning or end; indeed above reasoning. When consciousness of the Spirit manifests itself, man becomes free from the jaws of death.*
>
> Upanishads
> circa B.C.E 800

*Sa Ham* = She (Sa) I am (Ham) is also used.

## The Movement of the Left Ring Finger

You are no doubt aware that the left side of your brain controls the right side of your body, and the right side of your brain controls the left side of your body.

Although you can touch the thumb tips and forefingers of both hands together to form Gnana Mudra, I only want you to move the *left* ring finger in synchronization with the breath and mantra. By doing this we are ensuring, or at least encouraging, a slight dominance of the right hemisphere which expresses in rhythm, music, imagery, and feeling.

*In the world's audience hall, the simple blade of grass sits on the same carpet with the sunbeams, and the stars of midnight.*

Rabindranath Tagore
1861–1941

The problem for Westerners is that we are lopsided or "half-witted," and our whole education system places us into a limited perceptual mode. The nature of our mindset is analytical—we are trained to perceive differences and consequently wonder why life seems so fragmented! This is precisely the natural function of the left half of our brain, which knows only analytical, verbal, linear, and rational processes.

Eastern, and, therefore, Indian thought processes, favor analogical comparisons of similarities rather than differences and it is this mode that the right hemisphere of our brain operates from.

We need, in our meditative practices, to sacrifice understanding for *experience* and logic for *being!*

## Meditation Tip

When you commence meditating, you can try balancing a book on your head, which will act as an alarm clock. The book will drop from your head as soon as you lose control of your neck muscles and slip into a dreaming mode—this can alert you to be more conscious and maintain a *waking dream* state.

## Gayatri So Hum Meditation Technique

Remember that anything under thirty minutes is a waste of time, and what I am sharing with you is from my heart—how much from the heart we will discuss at the end of the next chapter!

## Technique Summary: ARRTM

- Awareness of spontaneous Respiratory inspiration and expiration
- Recitation mentally of "So" on inspiration and "Hum" on expiration
- Touch together the thumb and forefinger of the left hand (both hands if you wish) to form Gnana Mudra
- Move gently the ring finger of the left hand toward the base of the thumb on inhalation and away on exhalation

# 6

# Possibilities at Death

THERE ARE AT LEAST SIX POSSIBILITIES THAT can happen to the spiritual body at death:

- Earthbound
- Possession
- Trapped in the Astral Body
- Instant Replay
- Reincarnation
- Freedom

## *Earthbound*

The number one possibility at death is a phenomenon with which I have had a lot of personal experience—the haunted house. In Western esoteric tradition that would be called *earthbound*. The earthbound state invariably occurs with individuals who have died under particularly violent, horrible or depressing circumstances. What happens is that the astral body clings to the actual physical location of the death.

Yes, there are haunted houses in England, and there are haunted houses in every country around the world, but do you know what? You are crazy if you think a ghost can hurt you! A ghost can no more hurt you than my projector film can hurt you. What can hurt you is your mind—your reaction.

Dead people! I have talked to stacks of dead people. I've been with lots of people when they have died. I have talked to many of them after they are dead. Nobody can hurt you—there is nothing to fear but fear itself!

But let's get back to haunted houses. If someone dies—particularly a horrible death, or a depressing, lonely death—they stay there, they will not let go, they do not even know they are dead, in fact.

What happens is that the astral body slowly disintegrates. It disintegrates in the place where the person died instead of moving on to what in Hinduism, is called a *loka* or a plane. This disintegrating astral mind impregnates the walls of the building.

Just as cassette players have a magnetic tape that has been impregnated, so in a haunted house a recording of the dead person's emotions locks into the structure of the building.

People may go on comfortably living in the house for years with no problems, when suddenly a new person moves in who becomes a catalyst without realizing it. He or she just walks into the place and *pop* . . . suddenly stuff starts happening. Some people have the ability to unconsciously manifest psychic traces, as if there is a hidden automatic tape recorder and they have activated the playback button.

All you are getting with a haunted house is the memory of the astral shell coming out of the walls where it is glued and making a fuss. So what do you do with a cassette tape when you want to clean it? You run it through a bar magnet device called an audio-cassette eraser, and poof—it's erased!

We went through a phase that some of my students will remember, about fifteen or sixteen years ago, when Rae Jones became a rather famous Australian poet. Jones had a nose for haunted houses; he would call me up at all hours and we would go out here, there, and everywhere around Sydney.

I worked with a girl at that time who was an excellent medium. She was an excellent medium because I could turn her on with Power Mantra and she could get in contact and then I could turn her off and go and have coffee. She would not worry about it, but other people would get very worried about it—it would be very bad for their mental health. She and I did all kinds of psychic work together, including *site seances*.

We cleared a house out in Balmain where a woman had spent six months alone dying of cancer. We walked into the living room in midsummer and so help me, it was freezing. In the kitchen, even with the sunlight streaming through the windows, the temperature was still freezing.

When you are dealing with dead people haunting houses, you have to get in touch with them—and they are just like you and I. You and I are often very neurotic. A ghost in a house is just a neurotic ghost. A live neurotic or a dead one, they are just the same. You use the same counseling procedures and coax them around, talk it out, and release some emotion.

We have Shakti Mantras (power sounds) that disintegrate spirits. That's it! Boom! Once we had disintegrated the entity in the house in Balmain, then the temperature immediately went up. The people who lived there could not believe it. For two years they had lived with a horrible eerie feeling and with odd things happening. The place was always cold and then the temperature just went up! I have had several personal experiences like that.

One possibility is that after death, if someone wants to communicate or something hasn't been resolved, they (the dead) can insert themselves in the walls, literally, and come out whenever possible, when someone acts as a catalyst-medium.

Although a dead remnant of someone's astral-emotional self may manifest, it can't hurt you, unless you think it can! Who was ever killed (except by fright) from a bit of talkative fog wafting around?

## Possession

There is a second possibility, but I have never seen a genuine case. That possibility is *possession*. I've handled a few such *apparent* cases with Power Mantra or Shakti Mantra.

Possession occurs when, after death, a person who is now in his or her astral-emotional body, with their mental and spiritual body locked in also, is unable to get away, and wishes to inhabit another physical vehicle for expression on this plane.

The disembodied psychic complex tries to find some living person who is in a mentally weak and vulnerable state. The dead being then proceeds to occupy a portion of the living being's mind. The result is two minds in one body—to everyone's disadvantage!

It is important to emphasize that such an event is *possible*, but *improbable!* Imagining that possession is a common occurrence and an explanation for everything that goes wrong is mentally unhealthy.

It is possible that such obsessing entities are just unwilling to go through the tedious business of reincarnating again into a physical body—I am a bit sick of being toilet trained myself!

Of the people who believe they are possessed, who go to spiritualists and exorcists and are told by these people that they are possessed, 99.99% show symptoms of either schizophrenia or what psychologists call multiple personality disorder. They can also be simple hysterics—however I can't disallow the possibility that there are genuine cases. I have dealt with a number of cases of possession, but I am not personally convinced that the incidents represented true examples of possession.

American psychologist D. Y. Cohen, Ph.D., a few years ago investigated the phenomenon of possession. He devised a differential diagnosis that seems to hold true.

In schizophrenia and multiple personality disorder, the voice or personality that emerges is usually extremely destructive, suggesting ideas of violence and exhibiting paranoia.

In a genuine, albeit rare, case of possession, the voice is very obsequious, polite, and encouraging. In a sense it suggests: "You are a great genius, you are not recognized. I am going to unfold your full potential so the world will appreciate you. I have come to unleash your ability and you will conquer the world," and so on.

The entity is ever-busy, putting megalomaniacal ideas into the person's head, very slowly, at a reasonable rate, very polite, very nice. What they are trying to do is simply obtain another physical vehicle.

Possession is exceptionally rare. Most of what appears to be possession is schizophrenia and multiple personality disorder, but I can't dismiss the possibility. Many of you have your own ideas, your own viewpoints. I am merely teaching you a traditional pattern.

## *Trapped in the Astral Body*

The third possibility is that at death the etheric body leaves the physical body and the physical body disintegrates. The etheric body now begins to disintegrate, leaving us consciously trapped at the astral emotional body level.

The astral-emotional body goes to the so-called lower astral plane or loka and this is a world of magic because in this loka whatever is thought becomes *reality*.

Whatever is wished is immediately fulfilled! It is a dream world, a world of illusion!

There are many people who are dwelling in that astral world, in that world of illusion. Those who are dwelling in the astral world may need from one to six thousand years for the astral-emotional Kosha to disintegrate, thus freeing the mental and physical sheaths.

Such beings are repeatedly living out the moment of their death. They are like a record, stuck in one track, just one track, and are going over and over and over their death again.

There are a lot of young men who died in Vietnam who are in that astral world, still in the jungle, still firing.

## General Custer

You know who General Custer was in American history—where he fought his last great battle? We used to consider General Custer a fool, but lately we have learned that he was not. The Indians, it turned out, had the best repeating Winchesters, while the Army was still using old-fashioned carbines.

I offer this as an example, that General Custer is out there in that astral world fighting his last stand and there is a circle of Indians on the outside, going around and around him, and he is shooting and shooting. He is reliving it—without doubt. He was deeply engrossed in the battle, and so far as we know he did not have a deep philosophical intent other than to be a military officer.

The only thing true is that the Indians are on cardboard horses—they are made out of cardboard and they are firing cardboard ammunition, and General Custer is himself something like cardboard. It is complete Maya, complete illusion. When you get trapped in that afterworld, you believe it and you go over your death, over and over again.

## The Hashish Killers!

The eleventh century A.D. produced a Persian group that surely demonstrated that an *Idee fixe* (fixed idea) could carry you through death to plunge into an astral world of total illusion and delusion—and you would be willing to die for it!

The *Hashshashins* (Arabic for "Hashish eaters") were formed in A.D. 1090 by a legendary sheik known as "the old man of the mountain," and the offspring of his organization emerged in our contemporary world as *international terrorists*.

Our English words "assassin" and "hashish" both derive from this Islamic secret society that spawned the prototypes of today's suicide bombers.

The "old man of the mountain" initiated his members by drugging them with copious quantities of hashish and transporting them to a wonderful garden full of beautiful women who catered to their every desire.

After many hours of intoxicated pleasure they were then drugged unconscious and taken out of the garden. When they awoke they were told that they had actually visited paradise and if they murdered ruthlessly for the society and died in the mission, they would return to that paradise for eternity.

This experience produced brainwashed fanatics (the origin of *fan*), who did not hesitate to sacrifice their own lives with true religious fervor. Not for them some insipid Christian dream of clouds and harps—they got real live women! They wreaked havoc with the Crusaders who, on the whole, were a pretty brutal lot themselves.

I am certain there is many a Hashshashin still living in a total world of Maya—propelled there by tremendous emotion and belief at the moment of their death—they are sleeping with voluptuous store manikins, being served out of paper cups, and they haven't even noticed the "grapes" are plastic!

## Believing is Seeing

I'll give you some other possibilities of getting stuck in that astral world of complete total illusion. This also explains why someone may say, "Yes I met Paul at the pearly gates, and Jesus was there." If that is what they believe, that's what they've got. Somebody else says a great Master arrived and Aunt Molly was there. Quite right, they were, but it may be only an astral illusion. However, this is not to deny that you may contact your parents as you approach death and after death, nor to deny that your conception of deity will manifest in the form you recognize.

## *Instant Replay*

The foregoing were three possibilities. Now let me give you a fourth possibility. The fourth one has to do with the mental body. Remember, I said that the mental body could take over the stored memory from the astral body or from the cerebral cortex, if you wish. At death that mental body is capable of disgorging the entire life.

It is quite possible, under some circumstances, that what occurs is not reincarnation, but recurrence. You do not reincarnate—you recur—and that recurrence is a circle.

You can go into a loka where the mental body is naturally drawn, and you will not go over the moment of your death, over and over. Instead what you do is relive the entire record—that is, every groove of that record of your entire life from the moment of birth right around to the moment of death, in a normal time sequence. You can stay there anywhere from one to six thousand years before the record and the mental body break apart.

Do you remember Lao Tzu's puzzle? He fell asleep and dreamed he was a butterfly, and then he knew not who he was. Was he a butterfly dreaming he was a man, or was he a man dreaming he was a butterfly?

We confuse *sleeping* with being awake and being *awake* with sleeping—a Gurdjivian delirium, the horror of which, once comprehended, reduces Lao's butterfly conundrum to an understatement!

You do not know if you have not been in this very place for the hundred and fiftieth time, that this whole thing is not another illusion, that you just relive your whole life, every incident from birth to death, in three dimensions, live Technicolor, cinemascope. You are right there in it! Recurrence, in some esoteric schools, particularly Sufi and Ouspensky Fourth Way Traditions, is a very serious consideration.

We do not know whether every moment of our lives is simply a recurrence, that perhaps instead of being simply stuck on a track as in the astral plane, we are actually going through the whole record, all of the grooves, right to the center, and when we finish the record player automatically starts again, over and over again in an almost endless circle.

## *Reincarnation*

### The Incarnation Spiral

Now let us look at the fifth possibility.

That fifth possibility is probably the one that half of you would prefer to believe. I said half of you here, because it is an absolute fact that half of the world's population now adheres to the belief in reincarnation.

> *Everything that exists is in a manner the seed of that which will be.*
>
> Marcus Aurelius
> A.D. 121–180

Reincarnation implies not a circle, but a spiral that is either evolution or devolution, and it suggests that after death, as the Gita says, you will take upon a new body. Over half the world's population believes that.

Reincarnation also implies that our actions now bear fruit and shape subsequent incarnations. We do not find that necessarily easy to conceive or realize as causal connections are often hidden.

The first scientific evidence available is a book written over twenty years ago by Dr. Ian Stevenson, Professor of Psychiatry at the University of Virginia Medical School. *Cases of the Reincarnation Type: Ten Cases in India* (Charlottesville: University Press of Virginia, 1975) is still in print, or you can check it out at the Theosophical Society. Dr. Stevenson studied a dozen cases of reincarnation in detail and his conclusion is irrefutable. We are not arguing whether it is possible or not, I will just emphatically tell you yes, reincarnation occurs.

I have two caveats that I want you to consider—but you don't have to agree with me!

Do you have control?

First of all, the mistake I would suggest, or something worthy at least that you should keep in mind, is the popular idea of reincarnation automatically occurring. I suggest to you that recurrence is much more automatic than reincarnation—reincarnation *may* occur. Instead of just sitting back, enjoying life, and saying "Well next time around I'll do better," I would suggest to you that there are two big factors to keep in mind about reincarnation.

*In a seed, the tree which may spring from it is hidden; it is in a condition of potential existence; is there; but it will not admit definition. How much less, then, will those seeds which that tree in its turn may yield.*

Samuel L. Mathers
1850?–1918

Reincarnation may occur mainly by *accident!* The book written by the psychiatrist from the University of Virginia would suggest that more often than not, *reincarnation is an accident.* I would also suggest to you that past lives therapy, which is so popular and can be so useful, is frequently *unconscious fantasy,* and often does not stand up to investigation—the cases that do verify it are admittedly stunning, however!

The two major forms of reincarnation are:

- By accident
- By will

## Reincarnation by Intent

In the case of an Avatar, a Master, or you yourself, reincarnation can be achieved by will or intent. If you become self-possessed of will, reincarnation by Itcha Shakti (will power) may be accomplished, i.e. *you can reincarnate by adding the emotional fuel of desire to intent.*

Reincarnation by *intent* occurs when there has been strong desire and effort over a substantial part of the lifetime to achieve a particular goal.

This intent can be reinforced by the last few moments of life. If you are to achieve these last few moments, it is necessary that you concentrate correctly, and avoid becoming mentally scattered at the moment of death, or just before unconsciousness supervenes.

However, if other thoughts, not the intent, are in the mind at the time of death, it is not necessarily a problem. If the intent has been created and reinforced by previous desire and effort, then the intent emerges after death, regardless of the last few moments and thoughts.

It must be remembered that many of us will be on medication or be unconscious in the last few moments and that most Near Death Experiences happen to people who are deeply unconscious or under anaesthetic. It is the intent and actions over a longer period that are important.

Even if the thoughts of the last few moments of life are negative and contradictory to the intent, and provided that the intent has been actively worked toward during the lifetime, the intent overcomes the negativity of those last moments.

On the other hand, the attempt to become positive at the last moment of life, where good intent has not been part of the actual life, may be doomed to failure. Now is the time to prepare!

The thought of being on medication or caught in a difficult, last-minute situation need not perturb us, provided we are prepared. If the intent is strong because the appropriate thoughts and practices have been part of our lives, our path is secure. Hence the importance of a stable meditation technique as taught in the Meditation-Contemplation section.

## The Lama's Message

We experience a variety of attitudes from the very simple to the most profound when we contemplate death.

The year was 1982, and I was attending the Seventh International Transpersonal Conference in Bombay (now Mumbai), India.

I heard a wonderful Parsee teacher juxtapose the simple and the profound (Parsees worship *light*—not fire). He said: "Religion is an insurance in this world against fire in the next world, of which honesty is the best policy."

He contrasted the above statement with this: "Most believe at the moment of death the person dies and the Universe goes on, but could it be that the Universe dies and the person goes on?"

Much transpired that raised the obvious point that the East had a more mature and sophisticated awareness of death and dying.

One of the most poignant statements I ever heard was at the opening ceremony of this conference, when a message was read from the former Head Lama of the Tarab monastery in Kongpo, Tibet.

The Lama's letter read:

> I deeply regret my inability to attend as I have an unexpected and prior engagement.

And indeed he did! He was too ill to leave his bed—he was *dying!*

So all I am going to say about reincarnation is that it implies a spiral that is progress, evolution, or perhaps devolution—a downward spiral. I would suggest that you don't sit back and assume that reincarnation is the automatic answer, although half the world's population on the surface of the planet believes it is.

*The* ignorant *want personal survival after death, the* enlightened *desire impersonal survival after death.*

It occurs (a) by accident or (b) by design, and not everybody has the same lucky or unlucky accident, so if you want it you had better do some thinking and planning.

I am going to suggest that you can plan your next incarnation by preparing for it now!

You ask how? Decide what you want to do, study and actualize in your next life, then do everything you can to learn about it (even as a hobby) in this life.

## Freedom

Now I am going to mention the last possibility, which is beyond reincarnation, and that is Moksha or freedom. We want survival after death because most of us to a greater or larger extent are afraid of death. It is an experience we have not had—so we believe. Consequently we desire survival after death!

Moksha is that moment of meditation in which you can come together at death and the possibility exists of dissolving your etheric, astral, and mental bodies totally, so then only your spiritual body is left and the Purusha returns in one blaze to the Universal Sea from whence it came. What we confuse is Purusha, that soul or that self, with our life reincarnation.

*There are two ways of passing from this world—one in light and one in darkness.*
*When one passes in light, he does not come back; but when one passes in darkness, he returns.*

Bhagavad Gita
circa 400 B.C.

This Purusha (impersonal essence of self) is often called *Jiva* in Yoga, and is known as the *Atma* by Vedantists. It is the universal destiny of us all to return our Atma (the English equivalent words are "atom" and "atmosphere") to the cosmic reservoir as surely as the dew drop ultimately slips back to dissolve in the ocean.

Sri Gangaram Chagaubhhai Patel expressed this thought beautifully in a letter he shared with me:

> Many people turn to religion, and sometimes they get discouraged when they hear words from the Gita, which say that seekers of knowledge are very rare (one in thousands), and among the seekers of knowledge, perchance one really knows God. "If that is the case, then I do not have any hope of gaining knowledge," one may conclude. Actually, the truth is that it is everyone's destiny to gain knowledge of the Atma. When you turn an hourglass upside down, it will appear that, at any given time, not very many grains of sand are interested in going to the other side. But actually, they are all moving closer to the other side. And eventually, little by little, they all fall over to the other side.

## *Alchemy Laboratory — Phase 6*

### Exercise: Personal "Ultimate Priority" Lists

Everything we do in the alchemy laboratory is strongly transformational and transmutational. People who have NDEs often report that being able to separate the important from the unimportant has profoundly changed their lives. Patients informed that they have a terminal disease also report that life becomes lucid, *three-dimensional*, and meaningful for the first time.

> *All souls must undergo transmigration and the souls of men revolve like a stone which is thrown from a sling, so many turns before the final release. Only those who have not completed their perfection must suffer the wheel of rebirth by being reborn into another human body.*
>
> Zohar
> C.E. 120?–1200?

This is an exercise that is often mentioned, but seldom done by people who hear about it. The exercise is worthwhile doing, although most of us find it is quite difficult at first. It seriously forces you to face what is worthy of your attention in life and what really counts for you.

## My Personal "Ultimate Priority" Lists

You are going to die in three months. List nine priorities:

1.

2.

3.

4.

5.

6.

7.

8.

9.

You are going to die in three weeks. List nine priorities:

1.

2.

3.

4.

5.

6.

7.

8.

9.

You are going to die in three days. List nine priorities:

1.

2.

3.

4.

5.

6.

7.

8.

9.

You are going to die in three hours. List three priorities:

1.

2.

3.

## *The Inner Chat Room — 6*

Let us recapitulate the death process using slightly different terminology.

In the words of the great Hindu scholar, B. Bhattacharya, from his monumental work *Shaivism and Phallic World* (New Delhi: Oxford & IBH Publishing Co., 1975):

> Then is explained the process of final decay of mind and functions, known as death, and how it gradually operates in a way which leaves the conscious self free from death. The senses of a dying person get gradually disconnected from the outer world; they recede into the Mind. The mind fails to function externally, having lost its relating connections with objects. It functions in the subjects, however (memory and uninhibited reflexes of memory), and withdraws to Prana. Prana as a function now clings to the cause of this individual Prana, the identity, the Jiva. Now the Jiva has to leave the heap of decay. As it does, it carries Prana along with it. The Jiva's identity, like water to water, heat to heat, air to air, gets gradually mixed up with the five gross elements.

Thus we see that death is normally a gradual process that releases the conscious self, which is the *identity,* and this identity does not die.

When the identity, with its accompanying life force, leaves the body, so does the heat.

As a general rule, at this point there are two paths, rebirth or oneness with god (liberation from reincarnation), with the choice based on the identity's karmic energy (past deeds and practices).

However the path of reincarnation is not necessarily automatic within a time frame and a person's identity and accompanying life force may become lost in an illusion for six thousand years (according to certain teachings passed to me).

It is karma that provides both the energy to manufacture illusion and to cut through illusion.

*He (the Atman) dwells in the breath, he is within the breath; the breath, however does not know him; the breath is his body, he controls the breath from within.*

Brhadaranyaka Upanishad

The will (intent), along with the last thoughts and the de sires of the heart contribute to how the identity will progress.

If the identity is to attain oneness and has worshipped a god (e.g. Christ, Shiva), the identity merges with that god and attains liberation through that god. If the oneness is attained without a god but god-realization, the liberation is immediate.

# Meditation-Contemplation — 6

## Gayatri So Hum Meditation — Part 5

The classical schools of Indian philosophy link the individual self, soul, or essence, with the breath. Without making fine academic Sanskrit distinctions, a quick survey of the words used to denote the transcendental self is useful.

*The little space within the heart is as great as this vast universe. The heavens and the earth are there, and the sun, and the moon, and the stars; fire and lightning and winds are there; and all that now is and all that is not: for the whole universe is in Him and He dwells within our heart.*

Upanishads
circa 800 B.C.

*Atman* is the term most used by the Vedanta school. Atman implies breath and survives down the Indo-Aryan language tree as the German verb "to breathe."

Amazingly, Atman is associated with two words in English, although we normally identify these words as coming from the Greek. Our English "atmosphere" and "atom" are cognate terms with the Sanskrit Atman, and consequently the Vedantic philosophers often make a play on this by saying "Atmic power exceeds atomic power." We can also turn to India's Persian neighbors for some insight that predated the atomic era.

*Jiva* (literally "life monad") is the term most favored in the Yoga texts. Dr. Georg Feurstein, an Indologist well qualified to split hairs, comments in his superb *Encyclopedic Dictionary of Yoga* (London: Unwin Paperbacks, 1990):

> There is a close relationship between the Jiva and the life force (prana) as breath—a relationship that has been carefully studied in hatha-yoga. Thus, in the Goraksha-Paddhati we find...
>
> It (Jiva) leaves (the body) with the sound ha and it enters with the sound sa—both sounds being continually recited (and forming the ham-sa mantra).

Purusha is the Sanskrit word used by students of Samkhya; I prefer the translation of the word that states the self "sleeps within the city (body)" until we awaken with the kiss of focused consciousness.

> *The self is no more in the mind than the wind is in the trees.*
>
> Swami Anandakapila Saraswati
> *A Chakra & Kundalini Workbook*

The Purusha is the deathless, birthless, self-existent, eternal part of us; the great Indologist, Heinrich Zimmer, was fond of using the analogy that the Purusha is no more affected by what happens in our life than the Sun is affected by a forest fire on the earth.

*Split the atom's heart, and lo!*
*Within it thou wilt find a sun.*

Persian Mystic Poem

Both Shankaracharya (a Hindu reformist of the eighth century A.D.) and the Katho Upanishad place the Purusha, as a bright unwavering flame the size of the thumb, within the psychic correlate of the *heart*—i.e. Anahata Chakra.

Shankaracharya advocates meditation upon the Purusha as a flame within the heart cavity, and this is precisely what I was taught to do while performing the Gayatri So Hum. This is the last and final secret of the meditation method I am sharing with you, and I suggest that throughout the meditation, you visualize a pure white flame within your heart.

When you realize this is the final step, a new meaning to the significance of moving the left ring finger toward the base of the thumb appears. Throughout the Gayatri So Hum you are *bowing* with the left ring finger to your *higher self*.

Thus the true magnificence of this path becomes clear: every outgoing breath is the merging of the divine swan Hamsa with the absolute, and with every ingoing breath the absolute is merging with the individual self.

With each exhalation the microcosm, or little world of the self, goes forth to dissolve in ultimate reality, while with each inhalation the macrocosm, or universal ultimate reality, enters and suffuses our being.

All conscious practice of the sacred Gayatri So Hum reenacts the cosmic drama of expansion/ contraction, universe after universe, for eternity and throughout infinity.

With inspiration followed by expiration, the grand cosmic play is enacted both within and without, ceaselessly involving/evolving the essence that is truly us.

The implications of the Gayatri So Hum meditation are profound and wonderful. That which is within goes without, and that which is without goes within.

The ancient Upanishads and the Hindu sages, such as Goraksha, revealed a profound mystery when they expounded the Gayatri So Hum; this meditation truly carries us through the ocean of infinite and eternal cycles.

## Meditation Dip

A natural dip occurs in the human biorhythm between 3:00 P.M. and 7:00 P.M. Hence the optimum time to recoup your energies and assimilate the activities of the day (which is the function of dreaming) is sometime within that afternoon to early evening time frame.

This 3:00 P.M. to 7:00 P.M. low is of major concern to industrial psychologists, as it has been discovered this is the major period for serious car and truck accidents. This is not due to heavy traffic flow, but rather a function of driver fatigue—individuals literally drop off at the wheel for a few seconds.

## Technique Summary: HARRTM

- The heart is to be visualized as having a pure white flame burning within it throughout the meditation
- Awareness of spontaneous
- Respiratory inspiration and expiration
- Recitation mentally of "So" on inspiration and "Hum" on expiration
- Touch together the thumb and forefinger of the left hand (both hands if you wish) to form Gnana Mudra
- Move gently the ring finger of the left hand toward the base of the thumb on inhalation and away on exhalation

# 7

# LIFE AND DEATH: THE SAME COIN

> . . . the antithesis of any given thing confers meaning upon it. Light is insignificant without darkness, and life is meaningless without death."
>
> *Ecstasy Through Tantra*

## *Life after Life*

Let me sum up the whole thing. If you are a surfer, you go to the beach and you have seen waves roll in.

Let's take each wave as a life—that is, it has a birth, it has a beginning, it reaches a crest, and then it goes down into a valley. So we mistake the waves for life after life.

Now our illusion, when we are on the shore, is that the wave that we see forty meters out is the same wave that dashes itself on the beach. Not so! Waves are not individual, they are movements of water—undulations created by a force.

> *We are like the sea, people are waves; necessarily we are associated with everyone.*
>
> Ni'matullah Wali 1331–1431

That force is the Purusha, a force of conscious energy that goes through the universe, creating individual waves. In each wave, which we think is a life, is encompassed the personality compounded of the astral and mental body. Then that dies and the force continues on. The next life comes about, and there is an astral mental body complex, and that dies, and there is another astral mental body complex.

The true reincarnation, the purest reincarnation, is of the Purusha—not the personality or the mask. Now how do we put this all together?

## *The Secret of Death*

In the Katho Upanishad, a young boy whose father is a priest, goes to the god Yama (Yama is the god of death).

He says, "Oh Yama, teach me the ultimate secret of death."

Yama replies, "No."

Yama offers the boy everything—palaces, wealth, power, women—but the boy ignores Yama and immerses himself, doing Tapas (austerities and meditation) day after day.

The boy refuses all Yama's gifts until, in the end, the god of death is so moved by the boy's sincerity that he teaches him the secret of life. The secret of life is then the secret of death, and thus Yama initiates him.

> *Shun praise. Praise leads to self-delusion. Thy body is not Self, thy SELF is in itself without a body, and neither praise or blame affects it not.*
>
> H. P. Blavatsky
> 1831–1891

Life and death are the coins in our pocket. We take out the coin, it has a head and a tail. Life and death are the same coin, the one is the other and the other is the one and you do not know which is which. We do not know if this is illusion at this very moment, Maya. The ultimate secret of death is that: as in life, so in death.

How else could it be? As a man thinketh, so he is. Exactly as you conduct your life, so will your death be. If you are full of illusion in life, your death will be full of illusion. If you have enlightenment in life, you will have enlightenment in death.

## Your Thoughts are Your Reality

As a man thinketh, so he is. As a man willeth, so can he be. That ultimate secret that Yama gave the boy is that whatever you believe will be so in death.

If you believe Aunt Mary and Jesus Christ are going to be there, guess what—they will! If you believe Lord Buddha is going to be there, guess what—he will!

> *If a man's mind becomes pure, his surroundings will also become pure.*
>
> Buddha
> 568–488 B.C.

If you believe you are a bad person and deserve to go to hell, guess what—you will! There will be little red devils running around dancing in red paper flames, blown by fans, with paper pitchforks picking at you, and you will be screaming as though it is real pain—yet it is all illusion.

If you want to reincarnate, and you can pull yourself together and control your life, then you may be able to control your death and pick your reincarnation.

If you know that there is a danger of being lost in the astral world, in a world of illusion, and you can learn to avoid illusion in this life, then the possibility of avoiding illusion after death exists.

If you believe that when you die you really will be dead, i.e. oblivious, then you have the rest of your life. That's great! Have you ever had a deep dreamless sleep? Wonderful! And if you believe you want to take that deep dreamless sleep further and dissolve totally, then you have the potential to be totally and absolutely free!

> *As I pass from this world to the next, I know that heaven or hell is determined by the way people live their lives in the present. The sole purpose of life is to grow. The ultimate lesson is learning how to love and be loved unconditionally.*
>
> Elisabeth Kübler-Ross
> *The Wheel of Life: A Memoir of Living and Dying*

Unfortunately, I have not evolved that far. I still have some material wants and desires and unfinished business, so I am going to make it my business to come back. I am a bit mischievous—I can't resist the temptation yet—however I am getting close.

If you want to come back, you can pull your life together. If the life is pulled together before you die, *then you can pull it together after you die.*

Here is the very last thing I want to tell you. Elisabeth Kübler Ross, the Swiss psychiatrist was asked, "Why are people afraid to die?"

Her answer was: "Because they never lived."

That is brilliant. Who wouldn't be afraid to die if they had never lived?

> *For hatred does not cease by hatred at any time: hatred ceases by love—this is an old rule.*
>
> The Dhammapada
> circa 300 B.C.

And I want to say to you: stop worrying about reincarnation and double check that you have begun to incarnate!

If you make very sure that you are incarnating, then the reincarnation or whatever you want will look after itself. You may not be concerned with life after death, but what I am concerned about, and I suggest you be concerned about, is *life after birth*. The rest will look after itself.

## *Alchemy Laboratory — Phase 7*

We are going to perform a very important experiment in our imagination. The results may well put a new perspective on everything.

To understand the deep context in which this is placed, let me share three preliminary thoughts with you:

- The ancient Egyptian word for "womb" is the same as for "tomb"—one concept is synonymous with the other
- The Sanctum Sanctorum (Holy of Holies) in a Hindu temple is where the God or Goddess is placed and it is called the *Garbha-Griha,* or "Womb House"; Hinduism views the womb as sacred and the place of Divine beings.
- Primitive man, twenty to thirty thousand years ago, buried the dead in mother earth—which was literally their earth mother; they placed the dead on their side with the knees drawn up under the chin; this is the fetal position—the position of birth; can we assume that our instincts tell us that death is a beginning, not an end?

The following technique is reminiscent of Tibetan and Hindu Tantric meditations, but in fact I learned this from the famous British psychiatrist, the late R. D. Laing. I have done this with many groups and it usually has a fairly profound effect—it tends to induce quite a shock as you brush up against reality.

In a moment I am going to ask you to close your eyes. Do not open them until you have completed the exercise—this may include finding you cannot reach a satisfactory conclusion.

Let us pretend you can choose your next incarnation and this involves selecting your mother. The womb you will elect to incarnate in, and live within for nine months, must belong to someone you know who is already *incarnate in this life!*

Close your eyes and review every woman you have met who is currently alive and a potential candidate. Try to imagine what it would be like to be living inside the alchemical crucible of her womb.

See if you can find someone whom you would you feel comfortable about and trust?

Once you close your eyes, give this technique a good ten minutes. Whatever you get out of it is whatever you get. There is no *right* answer.

## *The Inner Chat Room — 7*

Now we are ready to integrate an ultimate meditation which classically is intended to carry you through the rest of your life up to and including the rest of your life that we call death.

> *In dream consciousness . . . we make things happen by wishing them, because we are not only the observer of what we experience but also the creator. In our creativity we prolong the magic action of the Creator of All in the overflow of His imagination, which is all that reality is, or ever will be.*
>
> Pir Vilayat Inayat Khan
> born 1916

The object of my meditation techniques, including the one I have been teaching you, is to experience deep relaxation and resuscitation of your body and your inner being.

I cannot emphasize enough that *this meditation is intended to provide a psychic and mental refuge* that will allow you to restore yourself daily. Meditation should be a pleasure, not a strain, nor work, nor something you dread having to do as a duty. The following points are the two key criteria by which you can judge your progress in learning to relax into meditation:

- Feeling that you are about to lose control of your neck muscles when you are sitting up
- The emergence of spontaneous dreams and visions and the feeling that you are on the borderline of sleep, yet not asleep

This meditation state of dreaming while sitting up is the *Bardo* or astral world of the Tibetan tradition and the psychic area where we can gain control, life after life.

> *The Indians may seem poor to we rich Westerners but in matters of the spirit it is we who are paupers and they who are millionaires.*
>
> Mark Twain
> 1895
> quoted by Michael Wood in his documentary series *Legacy*

Remember that the preliminary goal of the techniques I teach is always refreshment of body and soul in this life—now! Your meditation is a portable cocoon into which you may retreat anywhere, anytime, to emerge restored and renewed as the *psyche* or butterfly.

The Gayatri So Hum meditation is a gift of inner abundance from Hindu civilization to the West.

## *Meditation-Contemplation — 7*

### Gayatri So Hum Meditation

This is a very beautiful way of meditating that involves a steady visualization and three gentle synchronizations involving thought, breath, and movement:

1. Close your eyes and imagine, visualize, or feel a pure white flame in the center of your heart. Do not worry about whether this is a perfect picture—it is the willingness to see that is important. This is the eternal flame of which the temple *jyoti* lights are the outward representation.

2. Awareness of your spontaneous, uninhibited, uninterfered-with breath cycle of inhalation and exhalation. The breath is only observed, never volitionally controlled!

3. The mental repetition of the classic mantra So Hum with your breath cycle so that you silently say "So" as your breath flows spontaneously in and silently say "Hum" as your breath flows out.

4. The synchronized movement of the ring finger toward the fleshy mound at the base of your left thumb with the natural inhalation of your breath and the gentle movement of the finger away from the base of the thumb as your breath spontaneously flows out.

You proceed to unite the movement of your left ring finger with the inflow and outflow of your breath, and also harmonize the So Hum mantra. This is a yoking of breath, body (finger movement), and thought (mantra) that is truly classical Yoga.

The goal is refreshment through:

- Relaxing sitting up
- Dreaming sitting up
- Sleeping sitting up

When you are conscious of yourself snoring, this is a special state.

This is a very special Karma Shakti Kriya that gently coaxes you into the interior beautiful depths of yourself. A variation of this Kriya (Haung Sa) was a favorite of the great Yogananda (founder of SRF) and his disciple Swami Kriyananda.

The movement of the left ring finger *bowing* toward the mound of the thumb, and then withdrawing with the release of your breath, takes up immense slack in your mind and reduces agitation. Psychically this is a very special thing I am asking you to do and to understand this we need to consider an aspect of Indian Palmistry (some say palmistry originated in India).

The left ring finger is sacred to Surya (the creative power of the Sun—Apollo in Western palmistry), and very specifically to Anahata Chakra, or the

Heart Center. The fleshy pad at the base of the thumb is known as *Shukra's mount* or the mount of Venus. Symbolically, when you do this meditation you are opening your heart center to universal love, which is the alchemical solvent that dissolves Karma.

Notice that when you get very relaxed, the breath may almost cease. Both Swami Gitananda and Yogananda taught that this *Kewali Kumbhaka* or spontaneous cessation of breath, was a very positive sign of deep metabolic rest.

Be aware that your ring finger's gentle movement to and fro may spontaneously cease also. If you feel yourself coming out of the meditation you can re-instate the finger movement to take yourself back in. In *A Chakra & Kundalini Workbook* (p. 134), I explained:

> The famous *Gnana* (Pronounced: "G-yan" with the "g" as in "golf") mudra formed by joining the thumb and forefinger, leaving the remaining three fingers gently extended, demonstrates the anatomical, neurological, and psychological principles of mudra. Gnana mudra means literally "the wisdom gesture." The Sanskrit Gnana gives rise to Greek gnosis which comes through into English as *knowing*. The person who meditates in Gnana Mudra affirms a subsuming of all the wisdom of the universe, thus placing the mind automatically in an optimum state for higher consciousness.

In one system of symbology, the thumb represents the human, i.e. Purusha, the essence, while the forefinger is Brahman, the absolute source or matrix of existence. The remaining three fingers encompass all of manifestation as seen through the eternal principle of trinity: i.e. Brahma (creation), Vishnu (preservation), Shiva (changer), or God: G (eneration), O (rder), D (issolution).

> *Seated in a desert place, exempt from passion, master of his senses, let man represent to himself this spirit, one and infinite, without allowing his thoughts to stray elsewhere. Considering the visible universe as annihilated in spirit, let a man, pure through intelligence, constantly contemplate the One Spirit, as he might contemplate luminous ether.*
>
> Shankaracharya
> circa A.D. 900

In the final analysis, the Gayatri So Hum (referred to in the classic medieval text *Gherand Samhita* also as *Ajapa Gayatri*) is the pearl of meditations.

With expiration of (Hum) the Atman, the little self flows out to merge with the cosmic Paratma; and we die! With inspiration (So) the Cosmic Consciousness (Paratman) flows back within us, carrying the Jiva, or life force monad, to rekindle our life (reincarnation).

Thus, through our breath we are in constant contact or union with the Cosmos and each other. Gayatri So Hum is the path of realization, Samadhi, Cosmic Consciousness, and self-actualization.

And with that—*Hari Om Tat Sat.*

## *Appendix 1*

# RELEASE INTO LIGHT: MEDITATIONS FOR THOSE WHO MOURN

## *A presentation of The Theosophical Society in Australia*

**Used with Permission**

*Birth is not the beginning. Death is not the end.*

— Chuang-tsu

*It is clear to me as daylight that life and death are but phases of the same thing, the reverse and obverse of the same coin. In fact tribulation and death seem to me to present a phase far richer than happiness or life . . . . Death is as necessary for a man's growth as life itself.*

— Mahatma Gandhi

*Let life be beautiful like summer flowers and death like autumn leaves.*

— Tagore

*If you would indeed behold the spirit of death, open your heart wide into the body of life. For life and death are one, even as the river and the sea are one.*

— Kahlil Gibran

*Men who have seen life and death . . . as an unbroken continuum. The swinging of an eternal pendulum, have been able to move as freely into death as they walked through life. Socrates went to the grave almost perplexed by his companions' tears.*

— Voltaire

*The thought of death leaves me in perfect peace, for I have a firm conviction that our spirit is a being of indestructible nature; it works on from eternity to eternity; it is like the sun, which though it seems to set to our mortal eves, does not really set, but shines on perpetually.*

— Goethe

*Awareness of approach to death can be a beautiful thing, a frame into which we can put the work of art that is our life, our personal masterpiece.*

— June Singer

*Whether it is seen in personal terms or transpersonal terms, whether it is heaven or nirvana or the Happy Hunting Ground or the Garden of Paradise, the weight and authority of tradition maintains that death is just an alteration in our state of consciousness, and that the quality of our continued existence in the afterlife depends on the quality of our living here and now.*

— John White

*We are not only given the body but we are given the ability to see beyond the body and to realize that we are not tied to it forever.*

— Anonymous

*The reality of my life cannot die, for I am indestructible consciousness.*

— Paramahansa Yogananda

*Never the spirit was born: the spirit shall cease to be never;*
*Never was time it was not. End and Beginning are dreams!*
*Birthless and deathless and changeless remaineth the spirit forever.*
*Death hath not touched it at all, dead though the house of it seems.*

— Sir Edwin Arnold

*The disembodied soul does not part with Nature when it leaves the earth-life but, rather, it rises to a plane of Nature which is fuller, richer and sweeter in every way than the best of which the earth dwelling soul dreams. The dross of materiality burned away by the astral vibrations, the soul blossoms and bears spiritual fruit in the new life.*

— Yogi Ramacharaka

*The breaking of forms which we call death releases the consciousness within for the new adventure of building for further growth.*

— Joy Mills

*These bodies of the embodied One, who is eternal, indestructible and boundless, are known as finite . . . [The embodied One] is not born, nor doth he die; nor having been, ceaseth he any more to be: unborn. perpetual, eternal and ancient, he is not slain when the body is slaughtered. . . . As a man, casting off worn-out garments. taketh new ones, so the dweller in the body, casting off worn out bodies, entereth into others that are new . . . . For certain is death for the born, and certain is birth for the dead: therefore over the inevitable thou shouldst not grieve.*

— Bhagavad Gita

*I wish there were a place for gracious dying.*
*A high place with a distant view,*
*Where we could gather for a celebration of life*
*And death and friendship, old and new,*
*I'd like a place where there would be good music,*
*Good food and wine—and laughter, games and fun—*
*And quiet talk with friends, and good discussion*
*Of what will happen when this life is done.*

— Helen Ansley

*In the great wisdom traditions we are told of a period of evaluation following the transition beyond life in physical form. It is told that as we cross into other levels of being, what we have to offer is the result of the choices of action we have taken throughout the time on earth. This is looked upon kindly by the guardians, allowing us to see the effects of our choosing and how, in certain instances, we might have chosen better. It is without harsh judgment but simply seeing clearly and with perception.*

— Anonymous

*Thou causest the wind to blow and the rain to fall. Thou sustainest the living with loving kindness, and in great mercy calmest the departed to everlasting life.*

— Jewish Prayer

*The more we know the more fully we trust, for we shall feel with utter certainty that we and our dead are alike in the hands of perfect Power and perfect Wisdom directed by perfect Love.*

— C. W. Leadbeater

*It is not this trivial self which remains. It is the higher self that is much more aware of the understanding of what we have experienced . . . . How sad it would be to bring back this [small self] when we could bring back the best of our traits, a cleaner slate and a better situation.*

— Anonymous

*Or ever the silver cord be loosed, or the golden bowl be broken, or the pitcher be broken at the fountain, or the wheel broken at the cistern. Then shall the dust return to the earth as it was and the spirit shall return to God who gave it.*

— Ecclesiastes

*What is perhaps the most incredible common element in the accounts of near-death experiences . . . is the encounter with a very bright light . . . . The love and warmth that emanate from this Being to the dying person are utterly beyond words, and he feels completely at ease and accepted in the presence of this Being . . . He is ineluctably drawn to it.*

— Raymond A. Moody

*Death is our sister, we praise Thee for Death*
*Who releases the soul to the light of Thy gaze:*
*And dying we cry with the last of our breath*
*Our thanks and our praise.*

— St. Francis of Assisi

*My beloved soul, having awakened at last into My Peace, you can now return consciously and completely to your own Original Source. As this homecoming fills you with inexpressible joy, it pervades Allah Most High with profound delight as well. [You will] experience the perfect union with Love that is My highest Paradise.*

— Lex Hixon

*In the old way, when it was time to die, old ones would go off by themselves, feeling that the moment of death was as intimate between them and the Earth Mother as the moment of birth is between human mother and child. They would find a quiet place and there make prayers to the Great Spirit, thanking him for the life they had enjoyed. They would sing their song, and they would die.*

— Sun Bear and Wabun

*I have got my leave. Bid me farewell, my brothers! I bow to you all and take my departure. Here I give back the keys of my door and give up all claims to my house. I ask only for the last kind words from you, We were neighbors for long, but I received more than I could give. Now the day has dawned and the lamp that lit my dark corner is out. A summons has come and I am ready for my journey.*

— Tagore

*I often think that people we have loved and who have loved us become a part of us and we carry them around all the time—whether we see them or not. And in some ways we are a sum total of those who have loved us and those we have given ourselves to.*

— Anonymous

*There are only two faces to existence—birth and death and life survives them both. Just so sunrise and sunset are not essentially different: it all depends on whether one is facing east or west.*

— Joy Mills

*In the face of such a mystery, we need to tread gently and respectfully . . . . As far as is humanly possible, it is the business of the living to help the dying to die a natural death in a way that is in keeping with death's beauty and grandeur.*

— Catherine Roberts

*Great Spirit,*
*When we face the sunset*
*when we come singing*
*the last song, may it be*
*without shame, singing*
*it is finished in beauty.*
*it is finished in beauty!*

— Evelyn Eaton

*Letting the last breath come.*
*Letting the last breath go.*
*Dissolving, dissolving into vast space, the light body released from its heavier form. A sense of connectedness with all that is, all sense of separation dissolved in the vastness of being. Each breath melting into space as though it were the last.*

— Stephen Levine

*Words and tears are nature's most basic ways of helping us release our feelings of suffering.*

— Hospice of DuPage

*There are many levels of life which we cannot see and know and yet which certainly exist. There is a larger world, vast enough to include immortality. Our spiritual natures belong to this larger world . . . . If death is apparently an outward fact, immortality is an inner certainty.*

— Manly P. Hall

*Let us not cling to mourning,*
*Do not stand on my grave and weep.*
*I am not there*
*I do not sleep.*
*I am a thousand winds that blow,*
*I am the diamond glints on snow,*
*I am the sunlight opened grain,*
*I am the gentle autumn's rain.*
*When you awaken in the morning's hush*
*I am the swift uplifting rush*
*of quiet birds in circled flight,*
*I am the soft stars that shine at night.*

*Do not stand on my grave and cry.*

*I am not there*

*I did not die.*

— Anonymous

# *Appendix 2*

# THEOSOPHICAL SOCIETY

THE THEOSOPHICAL SOCIETY IS AN INTERnational organization dedicated to the promotion of brotherhood and to the encouragement of the study of religion, philosophy, and science, so we may better understand ourselves and our place in the universe.

The Theosophical Society has no dogma and stands for complete freedom of individual search and belief. Therefore, the ideas expressed in its publications are not in the nature of official statements. They are offered to stimulate thought and to encourage study and inquiry.

For further information contact The Theosophical Society in Australia, at one of its major centers:

Adelaide
310 South Terrace
Adelaide, S.A. 5000
(08) 8223 4877

Brisbane
355 Wickham Terrace
Brisbane, Qld. 4000
(07) 3839 1453

Hobart
13 Goulburn Street
Hobart, Tas. 7000
(03) 6231 4454

Melbourne
126 Russell Street
Melbourne, Vic. 3000
(03) 9650 2315

Perth
21 Glendower Street
Perth W.A. 6000
(08) 9227 7757

Sydney
484 Kent Street
Sydney NSW 2000
(02) 9267 6955

For other centers contact the Australian Headquarters:

The Theosophical Society in Australia
4th floor, 484 Kent Street
Sydney NSW 2000
Phone: (02) 9264 7056
Fax: (02) 9264 5857

# Glossary

**AMORC:** Rosicrucian Order founded in the 1920s by Dr. H. Spencer Lewis, based on a mandate from the earlier European order.

**Anahata Chakra:** The energy center at the heart.

**Ananda:** Bliss; joy.

**Anandamaya Kosha:** See Kosha.

**Annamaya Kosha:** See Kosha

**Arachnid Mater:** Spider Mother; lining of the brain permeated with profuse spider-like webs of blood vessels.

**Arbor Vita:** Cerebellum; Tree of Life; the balance center of the body.

**ASC:** Altered states of consciousness.

**Atman:** Atman implies breath and survives down the Indo-Aryan language tree as the German verb "to breathe"; it is the term most used by the Vedanta school.

**Bhagavad Gita:** Textbook of Karma Yoga; Yoga scripture in the form of a story, probably the most famous; an episode in one of the two national epics of India, the Mahabharata (the other national epic is the Ramayana).

**Brahma Dandu:** A pole or staff used by Shiva Yogis in North India which is a representation of the human spinal cord.

**Brahma:** The Hindu God of Creation; one of the classic triad; the first element and the *generation* part in the "GOD" process—Brahma, Vishnu and Shiva—Generation, Order, and Disintegration.

**Buddha:** The founder of Buddhism (500 B.C.).

**Buddhism:** The eightfold path consisting of correct vision, correct resolve, correct speech, correct conduct, correct livelihood, correct exertion, correct mindfulness and correct concentration.

**DNA:** Deoxyribonucleic Acid; a complex molecule that is part of the chromosome and the carrier of the genetic code determining our inheritance.

**Dura Mater:** Hard mother; very firm protective tissue between the brain and the skull.

**Goraksha-Samhita:** A Yoga text was written in India about A.D. 1200, purportedly by a legendary Yoga master named Goraksha, containing the meditation technique based on the respiratory cycle, the technique called Gayatri So Hum.

**GSR:** Galvanic skin response. This is a measure of skin conductivity and therefore an index of stress or anxiety. The greater the skin conductivity, the greater the stress or arousal level.

**Hamsa:** The divine goose (*Anser Indicus*) a beautiful white bird eulogized in the ancient Hindu scriptures; the continuous unconscious mantric vibration, So Ham, but often written as Hamsa or Hansa.

**Hatha-yoga:** Type of yoga where the preparation for self-realization is attained through perfecting the body.

**Hindu:** A follower or an aspect of the Hinduism.

**Hinduism:** The dominant culture of India.

**Jainism:** The spiritual tradition founded by Vardhamana Mahavira, a contemporary of Buddha (500 B.C.).

**Jiva:** Mental fire; the psyche.

**Kali:** Derived from Sanskrit adjective meaning black or dark blue as well as from a noun meaning time and destiny; Indian goddess from whom we emerge and to whom we return in endless rounds.

**Kapila:** A contemporary of Buddha and the founder of Samkhya, one of the six classical schools of Indian philosophy (500 B.C.).

**Karma Shakti Kriya:** A program to clear karma in nine days; a powerful technique to burn off karma equivalent to a deep-frying of the seeds in your being that represent potential SaBija and Agami Karma; designed by Dr. Swami Gitananda Giri.

**Karma:** The law of psycho-spiritual growth that involves an equal and opposite reaction for every action.

**Kosha:** The five bodies of man taught by Yoga, Vedanta and Tantra which are physical body, (Annamaya Kosha), etheric body (Pranamaya Kosha), astral body Manamaya Kosha, mental Body (Vijnamaya Kosha), and spiritual body (Anandamaya Kosha).

**Kumbhaka:** Momentary pause or retention of the breath.

**Kumkum:** Red powder used in rituals for marking psychic points on the body; often used on the third eye center.

**Manamaya Kosha:** See Kosha.

**Mantra:** Power sound; mind tool derived from the Sanskrit prefix *man* meaning "mind" and the Sanskrit suffix *tra* meaning a tool or an instrument.

**Maya:** Illusion; phantom existence; illusion of life.

**Melatonin:** A chemical produced by the body attributed with prolonging life.

**Moksha:** Freedom from the cycle of death and reincarnation; liberation of the soul; dissolution of the mind.

**Mons Veneris:** The fleshy pad on top of a woman's pubic bone; literally the mountain of love; the fleshy pad forming the base of the thumb is the equivalent on the palm; the mountain where the Goddess of Love dwells; also referred to as Venusberg; in anatomy termed *Thenar eminence*.

**Nadis:** Pranic irrigation channels or acupuncture meridians that nourish the physical body; energy channels running throughout the body influencing circulation and metabolism.

**NDE:** Near Death Experience.

**Panchkona:** Five pointed star; the Pentagram.

**Paramahamsa:** Those whose souls feed only upon the purist of philosophical truths; title given to Yoga masters.

**Pia Mater:** Holy Mother; from the Latin *Pia Mater*; envelops the spiritual embryonic potential of man enshrined within the cerebrum or brain; the innermost membrane adhering to the convolutions of the brain.

**Pranamaya Kosha:** See Kosha.

**Puraka:** Inhalation of the breath.

**Purusha:** In Hindu tradition, the essence carried within the spiritual body.

**Rechaka:** Exhalation or expiration of the breath.

**REM:** Rapid eye movement.

**RNA:** Ribonucleic acid; a complex chemical found in the fluid of body cells concerned with protein manufacture.

**Rosicrucian:** see AMORC.

**Samkhya:** One of the six classical schools of Indian philosophy developed by the sage Kapila about the universe and life; the theoretical basis on which the practice of Yoga rests; the Laws of the Universe, including Karma.

**Samsara:** Flow; the eternal bondage of rebirth; the cycle of life and death.

**Sanskrit:** Ancient Indo-Arian literary language of India.

**Saraswati:** Indian Goddess; the mistress of music, arts and the bestower of wisdom; normally seen holding the Indian Lute (Veena).

**Shakti Mantras:** Power sounds

**Shakti:** Energy; Indian Goddess; female partner; personification of the divine; energy underlying manifest existence; the feminine counterpart of Shiva.

**Shiva:** Consciousness; static; Indian God; personification of the divine masculine (the female being Shakti). Third part of the Hindu trinity—the *disintegration* part of the process we call Brahma, Vishnu and Shiva G(eneration), O(rder) and D(isintegration).

**So Ham:** Sanskrit mantra pronounced So Hum.

**Sunyaka:** Momentary pause or suspension of the breath

**Tantra:** Web or weave, the weave without a weaver

**Turiya:** Yoga term for deep dreamless sleep, often accompanied by snoring where it is possible to retain.

**Upanishads:** A collection of sacred texts outlining the esoteric aspects of Hindu teachings; written after the Vedas.

**Vedanta:** The dominant of the six classical schools of Indian philosophy.

**Vedantists:** Followers of the Vedanta philosophy that originated with the Upanishads.

**Vijnamaya Kosha:** See Kosha.

**Vishnu:** Indian God; the order part of the process in Hinduism we call Brahma, Vishnu and Shiva—G(eneration), O(rder) and D(isintegration).

**Zen:** Japanese Buddhist school often equated with the mental aspects of Hindu Yoga; the word roughly translates as meditation.

# Bibliography

Bhattacharya, B. *Shaivism and Phallic World*. New Delhi: Oxford & IBH Publishing Company, Volume 1, 1975.

Engstrom, Dr. "Hypnotic Susceptibility Increased by EEG Alpha Training." *Nature Magazine*, 1970.

Fenwick, Peter and Elizabeth. *The Truth in the Light*. London: Hodders/Headline, 1995.

Feuerstein, Dr. Georg. *Encyclopedic Dictionary of Yoga*. London: Unwin Paperbacks, 1990.

Hopkins, Jerry, and Danny Sugerman. *No One Here Gets Out Alive*. New York: Warner Books, 1995.

Kübler-Ross, Dr Elisabeth M.D. *Death is of Vital Importance*. New York: Talman Co., 1995.

_____. *Healing in Our Time*. Barrytown, NY: Barrytown Ltd., 1997.

_____. *Living With Death and Dying*. New York: Macmillan, 1997.

_____. *The Wheel of Life: A Memoir of Living and Dying*. New York: Scribner, 1997.

Moody, Dr. Raymond, M.D. *Life After Life*. New York: Bantam Books, 1977.

Morse, Dr. Melvin, M.D. *Transformed by the Light*. New York: Ivy Books, 1992.

Mumford, Dr Jonn. *Ecstasy Through Tantra*. St. Paul: Llewellyn Publications, 1987.

_____. A *Chakra & Kundalini Workbook*. St. Paul: Llewellyn Publications, 1994.

_____. *Magical Tattwas: A Complete System for Self-Development*. St. Paul: Llewellyn Publications, 1997.

_____. *Mind Magic Kit*. St. Paul: Llewellyn Publications, 1998.

_____. *Psychosomatic Yoga*. London: Thorson's, 1974.

Stevenson, Dr. Ian. *Cases of the Reincarnation Type: Ten Cases in India*. Charlottesville: University Press of Virginia, 1975.

Stutley, Margaret and James. *A Dictionary of Hinduism*. London: Routledge & Kegan Paul, 1977.

Tigunait, Dr Pandit Rajmani. *From Death To Birth*. Honedale, PA: Himalayan Institute Press, 1997.

Walker, Benjamin. *Encyclopedia of Esoteric Man*. London: Routledge & Kegan Paul, 1977.

Zimmer, Dr. Heinrich. *Philosophies of India*. New York: Meridian Books, 1956.

# INDEX

## A



## B

## C



## D



## E



## F



## G



## H



## J



## K

## L



## M



## N



## O



## P

## BOOKS OF RELATED INTEREST FROM NAB

**THE GREAT MYSTERY OF LIFE BEYOND DEATH** — *Hiralal L. Kaji*

The varied experiences which a spirit undergoes after death are described in the book with clarity and verisimilitude, giving the reader a rare glimpse of another, unknown dimension. Professor Kaji's sincerity and veracity are patent. He laid no claim to supernatural powers, extrasensory perception or even a deep knowledge of the subject, and he disclaimed all responsibility for the views expressed. Regardless of its provenance, however, the book makes fascinating reading and will certainly provide food for thought, even for the most hardened sceptic.

**ISBN: 81-7822-138-1**

**LIVING MEANINGFULLY, DYING JOYFULLY** — *Geshé Kelsang Gyatso*

This inspiring book gives an unparalleled Buddhist insight into death and dying, helping us to develop an awareness of our own mortality in a way that will totally enrich and transform our human life. It shows us how to make the most of our human life, and explains what happens when we die and how we can face our own death without fear.

**ISBN: 81-7822-058-x**

**THE REINCARNATION CONTROVERSY** — *Steven Rosen*

This book is a thorough discourse on the science of reincarnation, and a most valuable book for any person who desires to know who they are, why things happen to them and what they can do to ensure a better life in the present and the future. As the embodied soul continually passes, in this body, from childhood, to youth, to old age, the soul similarly passes into another body at death.

**ISBN: 81-7822-175-6**

**PHYCHIC POWERS** — *Melita Denning* and *Osborne Phillips*

This practical guide offers complete step-by-step instructions on developing your innate psychic skills in divination, dowsing, clairvoyance, psychometry, and spirit communication. You will learn how to safely enhance your mental and psychic abilities, and to use your abilities to positively change your life and the lives of those around you. Psychic powers awaken your sixth sense, and you will be able to accomplish things you would never have believed possible.

**ISBN: 81-7822-051-2**

**PATH WITHOUT FORM** — *Robert Powell*

In this book, Dr. Robert Powell invites the reader to accompany him on his own adventures in self-exploration—a journey that spanned several decades and eventually led him to the ultimate teaching of the non-dual nature of reality. It describes the milestones achieved by the author on the path of deliverance with the hope. They may be of some help to others in their own emancipation.

**ISBN: 81-7822-135-7**

**TO BE AND NOT TO BE, THAT IS THE ANSWER** — *D.E. Harding*

This book explains how to uncover and tap the Infinite Core or Centre. The source of happiness, love and meaningful lives lies very much deep within ourselves. A life-changing and quite remarkable book. Practical, accessible, eminently readable, and while revealing fundamental and extraordinary truths, always imparts a sense of joy—even fun! The author is living evidence of the success of his methods—active, alert and full of energy at the age of 93!

**ISBN: 81-7822-106-3**

**THE MYTHS OF DEATH, REBIRTH, AND RESURRECTION** — *Joseph L. Henderson* and *Maud Oakes*

The tribal initiation of the shaman, the archetype of the serpent, exemplifies the death of the self and rebirth into transcendent, "unknowable" life. Henderson and Oakes trace the images and patterns of spiritual initiation in religious rituals and myths of resurrection, poems and epics, the cycles of nature, and universal human responses in art dreaming. The authors dramatize the metamorphosis from a common experience of death's inevitability into a transcendent freedom beyond the individual's limitations.

**ISBN: 81-7822-031-8**

**GOD THE ASTROLOGER** — *Jaffery Armstrong*

The book systematically reveals the lost links between religion, science, destiny, and free will. It is a clear guide to how the Divine actually manifests in the material world and how we can cooperate. It explains the true spiritual relevance of astrology in our lives and offers the profound revelation that God is the Original Astrologer. In short, the author discovered that astrology is not about fortune telling but, as Carl Jung suspected, it is deeper than psychology and is at the very basis of medicine. True astrology is the missing link between religion and science.

**ISBN: 81-7822-168-3**

**A NEW LOOK AT PAST LIVES: Deja who?** — *Judy Hall*

The book explores in depth the possible explanations such as collective memory, cryptamnesia, soul groups, accessing the Akashic Records and imprinting, and looks at the validity and relevance of past lives in this context. We are all fascinated with who we really are, where we came from and what the purpose of our life here on earth really is. This book can help us to understand many questions whether we believe these 'lives' to be true or symbolic or allegorical.

**ISBN: 81-7822-015-6**